Data-Driven Marketing with Artificial Intelligence

Harness the Power of Predictive Marketing and Machine Learning

By Magnus Unemyr
with contributions by Martin Wass

Data-Driven Marketing with Artificial Intelligence

By Magnus Unemyr with contributions by Martin Wass

1st of June, 2018

Amazon KDP (print edition) ISBN: 9781983059018

Amazon KDP (ebook edition) ASIN: B07D7FD1YM

Cover design and print version formatting: Bogdan Matei

Editing: Eric Anderson

All feedback welcomed: *feedback@unemyr.com*

TABLE OF
CONTENTS

Preface 11

How This Book is Organized 17

Introduction 23

    What is AI All About? 30

    Autonomous Marketing 31

    Key Terms 33

    Myths and Misconceptions 36

    Chapter Summary 37

How Does Marketing Software Use AI? 39

    Giving Your Company an Edge 41

        Competitive Intelligence 41

        Predictive Pricing 44

        Ads Strategy 46

        E-commerce and Omni-channel 48

        Business Anomaly Detection 50

        Contracts and Legal Agreements 51

    Content Marketing 51

        Content Strategy 52

        Content Creation 54

        Content Curation 57

        Content Repurposing 58

        Report Generation 59

        Public Speaking 59

    Lead and Customer Acquisition 60

        Sales Prospecting 61

        Conversion Ratio Optimization 62

        Attribution Modeling 65

    Customer Relationships 67

Email Marketing 67

Social Media.. 70

Chatbots.. 73

Customer Service... 78

Contact Enrichment.. 79

Knowing Your Customer 80

Customer Sentiment... 81

Churn Prediction and Customer Retention 83

Predictive Lead Scoring.. 85

Mass-Marketing and the Segment of One 87

Segmentation 87

Predictive Content and Personalization.......................... 88

Recommendation Engines 91

Audience Management.. 93

The Customer Journey.. 93

Cognitive Systems 95

Chapter Summary... 97

Build Your Own AI **99**

Use AI to Trigger Marketing Campaigns 101

Use AI in Software or Service Businesses 102

Use AI in Physical Products 104

The Structure of a Machine Learning System.................... 106

Chapter Summary.. 107

Big Data **109**

What is Big Data? 111

Data is the New Currency.. 113

Democratization of Supercomputing 113

Hadoop.. 114

Data Scientists 115

Chapter Summary.. 115

Predictive Analytics and Machine Learning **117**

Types of Models.. 120

Types of Learning 121

Work Process 122

Bias 125

Chapter Summary.. 126

AI Algorithms **127**
    Data Science and Technical Terms 130
    Regression 133
        Simple Linear Regression *133*
        Multiple Linear Regression *135*
        Logistic Regression *137*
    Classification 138
        Decision Trees *138*
        K-Nearest Neighbor *141*
        Naïve Bayes *142*
        Neural Networks *143*
    Clustering 146
        K-Means *146*
        DBSCAN *148*
        Agglomerative Hierarchical Clustering *150*
    Chapter Summary 151
Putting your AI to Work **153**
    Making Predictions 155
    Changing Conditions Require Retraining 156
    Continuous Retraining 157
    Hardware Accelerated and Distributed AI 157
    Chapter Summary 160
How Will AI Affect My Business? **161**
    Will AI Replace My Marketing Job? 163
        How to Position Yourself *166*
    Will AI Disrupt My Company or Industry? 167
    Chapter Summary 170
What's Next in Marketing After AI? **171**
    The Internet-of-Things 173
        Marketing Insights from Machine-Generated Data *173*
        Machines Becoming Customers *175*
        How do You Market to a Machine? *176*
        Let Marketing Data Control Machines *177*
    Blockchain 178
        A Trusted Ledger of Transactions *178*
        How Does Blockchain Apply to Marketing? *179*

Chapter Summary 180

Changes to the Society **181**

Ethics 183

Legal Matters and Explainable AI 185

AI Apocalypse? 187

Chapter Summary 188

Final Thoughts **189**

Please Review This Book **193**

Appendix 1: Traditional Data-Driven Marketing **197**

Key Marketing Metrics 199

Sales Indictors *199*

Churn *200*

Customer Lifetime Value *200*

Internet Marketing and e-commerce *201*

Predicting Customer Choice *202*

Marketing Automation 203

Segmenting *205*

Behavior Tracking *205*

Automated Workflows *207*

Integrating Data from Other Systems *208*

Using External Data *209*

Appendix 2: Vendor Interviews **211**

Albert 213

Bookmark 214

Conversica 215

Cortex 215

Crayon 216

Crimson Hexagon 217

Crobox 217

Cubed.ai 218

Dynamic Yield 218

Emarsys 219

Ignite 219

Lexalytics 220

MarketMuse 220

Motiva 221

Narrative Science 221

Nudge.ai 222

Ometria 222

Outlier.ai 223

Pathmatics 223

Perfect Price 224

Scoop.it.. 224

Sentient Technologies 225

Smart Moderation.. 225

TalkWalker 226

Vestorly.. 226

Supercharge Your Projects **229**

Feedback and Contacting the Author..................... **233**

Acknowledgements... **237**

PREFACE

Technology is transforming the marketing industry, and nothing will be more disruptive than artificial intelligence. I have read several books on how AI can be applied in marketing, but none captured a comprehensive review of the topic. They were all great books, but they focused on an area outside of my interests and background as a marketing executive. Some were too philosophical with little actionable advice for practitioners who want to get started with AI in marketing, while others were too technical, with hundreds of pages of mathematical formulae. I wanted to find a book that fell between these two extremes.

With over twenty years of experience in international marketing for the global software industry—including almost a decade as a vice president of sales and marketing—I wrote and published my first book on Internet marketing several years ago. I went on to write several books on marketing automation, digital marketing, and entrepreneurship, and used my experience from the software industry for a recent book on how the Internet-of-Things and artificial intelligence will transform the world.[1]

Drawing from this experience, this book is meant to sit between the extremes of philosophical and technical writing on AI. I believe it finds the right balance between an overview of marketing principles and the real meat on the bones of practical use, without going into mathematical detail. This is the book I would want to read if I were a CEO, CMO, or digital marketing manager seeking to understand AI-driven marketing for real business use.

---

1   *Mastering Online Marketing.* Available here: *https://www.amazon.ca/MASTERING-ON-LINE-MARKETING-automation-Entrepreneurship-ebook/dp/B0154B2FL6/*

The Internet of Things. Available here: *https://www.amazon.ca/Internet-Things-Industrial-Revo-lution-predictive-ebook/dp/B077RLMGSW/*

After reading this book, you will understand these key topics:

- The disruption that artificial intelligence and other emerging technologies will have on marketing, sales, and the industries that surround them
- An insider's look at the latest AI-based software tools and what they can do for marketers today
- AI and related technologies like big data, predictive analytics, and machine learning, and how they can be used in marketing
- How marketing is becoming data-driven and autonomous to a level never before conceived, replacing gut feeling with facts and insights
- How many marketing tools already use AI to improve marketing precision, efficiency, or cost effectiveness using predictive and prescriptive capabilities
- Why you might want to develop your own custom AI software, and how that is done
- Whether AI will put your job or business at risk
- How new technologies, beyond AI, might disrupt marketing even further
- The legal and ethical aspects of using AI

While we cover some complicated topics, I've made sure that the book is easy to understand for anyone interested in the field, even those without previous knowledge. I understand software and marketing quite well, but I am no data scientist or statistician. Thus, I am immensely grateful to my friend Martin Wass for contributing a chapter to provide an overview of AI algorithms in an accessible way. Martin is a professional statistician and data scientist, and he works to find valuable and almost invisible insights in oceans of data. He is the best resource I know for data science problems, and his contribution to this book has undoubtedly made it much better.

Please consider leaving an honest review on Amazon to help other readers. I would be most grateful. You can leave a review here: *https://www.amazon.com/Data-Driven-Marketing-Artificial-Intelligence-Predictive-ebook/dp/B07D7FD1YM*

Thank you for taking the time!

I also offer my services as a consultant on marketing automation and AI to help implement effective Internet marketing strategies into your business. Contact me at magnus@unemyr.com to discuss how I can help you meet your Internet marketing goals and take your company to the next level.

Finally, I invite you to connect with me on LinkedIn here: *https://www.linkedin.com/in/magnus-unemyr/*

And to visit my blog on marketing technology and AI: *https://unemyr.com/blog/*

Now, let's dive into the fascinating world of AI, where autonomous and self-optimizing systems turn science fiction into reality.

MAGNUS UNEMYR
Jönköping, Sweden. June 2018.

HOW THIS BOOK IS ORGANIZED

In the pages that follow, we will cover a broad range of topics in a natural and intuitive way. We begin with an overview of some basic concepts in artificial intelligence and its role in marketing, including the key terms you will need to understand this book. Then, we look at how AI can be applied for specific cases in marketing, including different applications of machine learning and other emerging technologies. Later, we explore the details of how AI systems are created and how your company can develop the tools to stay competitive with these innovative marketing strategies.

The book is organized into the following chapters:

- The **Introduction** gives an overview of artificial intelligence and its use in marketing, explains key terms, and sets the scene for following chapters. Here, we will bring you up to speed on what you need to know moving forward, whether you're new to the topic or an experienced digital marketer.
- **How Does Marketing Software Use AI?** This chapter provides an overview of how currently available AI systems can be deployed by purchasing commercial solutions. We look at what types of products are available and what they can do for your business.
- In **Build Your Own AI**, we explain why you might want to develop your own company-specific AI solution. We cover some helpful tools to get you started and an overview of the industry to help you choose the right approach.
- The chapter on **Big Data** provides a background to the data science technologies on which predictive analytics and machine learning are built. Understanding the basics of how

these systems work will help you speak more confidently about their implementation in your company.

- **Predictive Analytics and Machine Learning** goes beyond big data to look at how AI uses these massive amounts of information to create tools that would have been unfathomable a generation ago.
- The chapter on **AI Algorithms**, written by data scientist Martin Wass, provides an overview of popular AI algorithms and how they can be used to find unique insights in mountains of data. This insider's look at the backbone of AI shows the incredible complexity and ingenuity involved in creating these systems.
- **Putting your AI to Work** provides information on how self-learning prediction models can be integrated in your company's software. We'll look at the difference between a prediction system and a machine learning system, and how they can create a feedback loop that both generates data and uses it to improve its own operation.
- In **How Will AI Affect Me and My Business?**, we look at the risks your business faces due to these emerging technologies, and how you can improve your job security. Artificial intelligence is set to change the world dramatically, and it's important to understand what that will mean for you.
- **What's Next in Marketing After AI?** This chapter provides an overview of new technologies that may transform marketing in the years to come, once AI is commonplace. While many of these concepts will seem like science fiction, they are right around the corner and may be part of our lives sooner than you think.
- In **Changes to the Society**, we cover the ethical and legal issues related to artificial intelligence and machine learning. This is an increasingly important area of discussion as computers become able to provide autonomous decision making based on huge collections of data far more complex than a human could handle alone.

- Not everyone reading this book will be an internet marketing specialist. To help everyone understand the concepts and terms used here, we have added an overview of some established data-driven marketing tools and techniques in **Appendix 1: Traditional Data-Driven Marketing.** If you are new to this field or want to brush up before jumping into the book, you may want to start here.

- Finally, the bonus chapter in **Appendix 2: Vendor Interviews** includes highlights of recent interviews with leaders of some of the most prominent and emerging companies in the industry. Each section summarizes a longer interview that you can read in full on my blog.

INTRODUCTION

The marketing industry is being disrupted right before of our eyes. Artificial intelligence is transforming almost every sector, and marketing is no exception. It is and will continue to create a new world that is vastly different from what came before. Its prevalence will reach into nearly every part of our lives, and we can no longer afford to ignore it. Your competitors are already using artificial intelligence; now is the time to educate yourself and take action to give your company a competitive edge.

In May 2015, IBM's CEO Ginni Rometty made a bold prediction at the World of Watson event. "In the future, every decision that mankind makes is going to be informed by a cognitive system like Watson," she said. "And our lives will be better for it."

These are strong words, but IBM is effectively betting their company on AI, and so are many others. We are witnessing a disruptive technological revolution that is likely to have wider impacts than even the industrial revolution a century ago. We are at the precipice of a new world, and 2018 may well be the point in history that people will look back on as the point when the AI revolution truly began. We get to take part in this, to see it from the inside. It's an incredible opportunity.

Technical revolutions change the way we interact with machinery and open up vast avenues for future growth and innovation. From the invention of the wheel to Europe's industrial revolution, they bring about amazing social change and advancement. Manufacturing efficiency skyrocketed in the nineteenth and twentieth centuries with machines automating what was previously done with muscle alone. Electrification changed things again, this time enabling work without natural light. This helped to create an era of convenient consumer products that improve the comfort of our lives. The next revolution was in information technology, or IT, where automated data processing removed many manual and tedious tasks, particularly in offices. We are now entering the era of artificial intelligence, where analysis and decision-making are automated too. In fact, AI-guru Andrew Ng, co-founder of Coursera and adjunct professor at Stanford, claims that "AI is the new electricity." The world will never be the same again.

In the coming years, AI will work its way into every part of our lives, just as electricity did in the early twentieth century. How often are we away from electrical devices, even while sleeping? With a few exceptions, almost never. As this revolution continues and grows, AI will become just as ubiquitous. Already, we are using speech agents like Apple's Siri or Amazon's Alexa, and artificial intelligence are making marketing and business processes more efficient. Did you know that AI has already crept into virtually any part of marketing, including conversion ratio optimization, customer journey optimization, ad purchases, and even reviews of legal documents? No area of marketing—or business in general—will be untouched.

This is why investors and corporations are in an arms race to invest in or acquire innovative AI startups. In just one year, KPMG's Venture Pulse reports that venture capital investments in AI companies doubled from $6B in 2016 to $12B in 2017.[2]

Business leaders should pay attention. This is a time of enormous opportunities—and great risks. In fact, eBay CEO Devin Wenig declared in his keynote presentation at the ShopTalk conference in Las Vegas in 2017, "If you don't have an AI strategy, you are gonna die." AI will also profoundly change how businesses and customers communicate. For example, Gartner predicted that customers will manage 85% of their relationships with enterprises without interacting with a human by 2020.[3]

Still, most consumers are largely unaware of how artificial intelligence will affect their lives. A report by Sage reveals that 43% of US consumers and 46% of UK consumers have no idea what artificial intel-

---

2   Eileen Yu. "Asia VC Investment Clocks High of $15.6B," ZDNet. 18 January 2018. *http://www.zdnet.com/article/asia-vc-investment-clocks-high-of-15-6b/*

3   *Gartner Customer 360 Summit 2011, https://www.gartner.com/imagesrv/summits/docs/na/customer-360/C360_2011_brochure_FINAL.pdf*

ligence is about.[4] With AI profoundly changing how we live, this lack of understanding can be problematic, as myths and misconceptions about the technology can overshadow reality. AI isn't as threatening as some may think, though there are risks and problems most people haven't considered. Lack of knowledge may be a problem for society onwards.

AI will drive a massive shift in business models. In an AI-enabled and connected world, companies will have to adjust to new purchase patterns, or they will go out of business. This includes everything from subscription models to pay-per-use strategies, and may result in a winner-takes-all scenario where some companies control nearly all of the market. Entire industries are at risk of being wiped out as these changes become widespread, and the ones that survive will be radically different. For example, machines will soon begin making autonomous purchases in B2B and B2C contexts, changing distribution chains globally. We will look at all of this in detail a little later.

Gartner notes, "AI-derived business value is forecast to reach $3.9 trillion in 2022," and that "in the early years of AI, customer experience (CX) is the primary source of derived business value."[5] In other words, marketers are and will continue to be among the first to reap the benefits of AI. As this book will show, there is no shortage of innovative uses of artificial intelligence in marketing.

Adobe's CMO.com reported in March 2018 that "just 15% of enterprises are using AI. But 31% said it is on the agenda for the next 12 months. ... The impact of AI technologies on business is projected to increase labor productivity by up to 40% and enable people to make more efficient use of their time."[6] AI is set to significantly increase efficiency of advanced white-collar jobs in the near future—and remove some of them entirely.

4   "Survey Reveals Nearly 50% of Consumers State They 'Have No Idea What Artificial Intelligence is About," Sage, 2017. *https://www.sage.com/en-us/news/press-releases/2017/11/survey-reveals-nearly-50-percent-of-consumers-have-no-idea-what-artificial-intelligence-is-about/*

5   "Gartner Says Global Artificial Intelligence Business Value to Reach $1.2 Trillion in 2018," Gartner, 2018. *https://www.gartner.com/newsroom/id/3872933*

6   Giselle Abramovich. "Study Finds Investments in Customer Experience are Paying Off," CMO.com, 26 February 2018. *http://www.cmo.com/features/articles/2018/2/26/adobe-2018-digital-trends-report-findings.html*

Ray Kurzweil, one of the greatest futurists of our time, thinks machines will become smarter than humans by 2045, an event he calls the Singularity.[7] From that point onwards, machines will continue to outsmart us with an increasing intelligence gap, leaving us further behind and reliant on them. However, this doesn't mean the world will end. In fact, Kurzweil isn't particularly worried about this and sees AI as an opportunity for humans to grow and evolve.

However, another of the greatest futurists of our time—Elon Musk of Tesla and SpaceX—frequently warns us that AI could wield extreme levels of power that could very well be the end of humanity. He calls for legislation to limit the use of AI before things get out of hand. Whichever side you take on this, it's clear that once the powers of AI are out in the wild, they can't be put back into the bottle.

Whether a global threat or a new stage of human evolution, AI technologies signal a disruptive transformation. While we might take the boldest predictions with a grain of salt, AI is already upending the marketing industry—and most other industries too. Late entrants to AI-driven marketing may never recover, but early adopters will grow increasingly competitive. Artificial intelligence and machine learning run on data, and organizations with the most collected information are quickly creating an unfair advantage against smaller competitors with less data to process. This is why companies like Google and Facebook are gathering every conceivable piece of data on their users, even on topics that seem mundane. As we'll find out later on, with enough data to analyze, even seemingly unimportant information can become powerful.

Along with artificial intelligence, automation is coming to the marketing industry, and many are questioning the safety of their jobs. After reading this book, you might be able to answer that question, though to some, it might be frightening. Marketing is also becoming increasingly reliant on data science. It is becoming data-driven, and the old methods of working by intuition and gut feelings are being replaced with models that draw on facts. This enables self-optimizing and autonomous mar-

---

7   Dom Galeon and Christianna Reedy. "Kurzweil Claims That the Singularity Will Happen by 2045," Futurism.com, 5 October 2017. *https://futurism.com/kurzweil-claims-that-the-singularity-will-happen-by-2045/*

keting systems that would have been considered science fiction to most people only a couple of years ago.

The good news is that with systems built on new data science technologies, marketing can become more relevant and provide better customer experiences, thus improving customer loyalty and returns. For too long, marketing has been reliant on "spray and pray" methods that do little to create engagement. AI enables us to move from spammy and irrelevant mass marketing to personalized relationships again—but this time at scale. AI technologies will enable highly personalized precision marketing that is more efficient and provides far better customer experiences. However, these advantages are only possible for those with enough data to process, a forward-thinking mindset, and the right tools.

Scott Brinker is the VP of Platform Ecosystem at Hubspot and editor of the chiefmartec.com blog. On the topic of tools, he kindly gave me permission to reprint the 2018 edition of chiefmartec.com's legendary yearly marketing technology landscape infographic.[8] While it's difficult to read here, it demonstrates how complex the market has become. Check out the full version at the link listed in the footnote below.

According to chiefmartec.com, there are now almost 7000 different marketing tools on the market, up from only 350 just five years ago. Even

---

8   Scott Brinker. "Marketing Technology Landscape Supergraphic (2018): Martech 5000 (actually 6,829)," chiefmartec.com, 24 April 2018. *http://chiefmartec.com/2018/04/marketing-technology-landscape-supergraphic-2018/*

more interesting, Brinker removed predictive analytics as a category from the infographic this year. He explains the reasoning behind this change:

> *We got rid of the category for predictive analytics. It's not that predictive analytics capabilities have vanished. On the contrary, due to the huge explosion of machine learning in marketing, predictive features have been added to hundreds of products. In deciding not to have an artificial intelligence category — because AI is embedded in so many products across all martech categories — we realized that predictive analytics solutions would be better classified in the category of the capability they enabled (e.g., web analytics or sales intelligence).*

Regardless of how they are arranged, the sheer number of companies and tools in the market today is staggering. With the explosion of tools and ever-increasing applications, AI is becoming integrated into almost every aspect of marketing. Now, let's dive in to this fascinating world to give you a competitive edge in your market.

What is AI All About?

With artificial intelligence and related technologies, we can predict the future behavior of someone or something and determine how we should best respond to those insights. We can predict the probability of specific events; for example, if a blog post topic will perform well, the likelihood someone will buy a particular product, or whether a customer will defect or become loyal to the brand. Algorithms that predict the likelihood of something are called classification models in machine learning lingo.

We can also predict numeric values in any range, such as the predicted lifetime value of a particular customer, the best price for a product at a particular time, or the number of days before someone will make their next purchase. Algorithms that predict the amount of something are called regression models.

With clustering algorithms, we can predict group association. For example, which groups of customers spend most money, and what similarities do the customers in those groups have between each other? This is called auto-segmentation and can be used to create lookalike audiences as well, meaning groups who share similarities in demographics, behavior, or other characteristics.

In fact, artificial intelligence—or more accurately, machine learning—is mostly about making predictions. We do this by analyzing information we already have to determine something we don't know. In effect, we let the data speak to us. This is why we sometimes call it predictive marketing, or precision marketing. Making accurate predictions is great and can greatly improve your marketing efforts. However, we can take this one step further.

After predictions come prescriptions. With prescriptive systems, we not only get insights about the likelihood of future events, we also get recommendations on how to best respond to those insights. In other words, prescriptive systems tell us what to do next in a given situation. A prescriptive algorithm can, for example, chose which email content to send to a particular customer, and at what time the message should to be sent to maximize the chance of it being opened and read.

We can use predictive marketing to determine the most likely outcome of something, and similar technologies to determine the best response to those insights. These two capabilities are at the heart of these new technologies, and we'll look at them in detail in the coming sections.

Autonomous Marketing

Marketing is becoming increasingly autonomous, meaning more and more of the touchpoints with consumers are created or managed by an automated system without direct human intervention. On its own, this isn't new. We've had it for a while with marketing automation systems (see Appendix 1) that could nurture leads automatically and personalize content at basic levels. However, we are entering a world of fully autonomous marketing, and that is going to change everything.

Many marketing tasks like purchasing ads, optimizing campaigns, managing the customer journey, or redesigning a landing page as part of conversion ratio optimization (CRO) efforts are all human tasks that are now being replaced by AI-bots that do this faster and more effectively. The same goes for content strategy and SEO optimization, CRM data enrichment, customer service engagements using chatbots, social media moderation, and much more. Right now, we still need marketing teams, but they are increasingly being relieved of the grunt work of analytics to focus on the creative and strategic side of the industry instead.

It wasn't long ago that everyone was talking about having a "mobile-first" strategy, meaning that businesses focused on customers accessing their online assets and services from mobile devices more often than from desktop computers. Today, mobile-first strategies are for laggards. We are now entering the "AI-first" world, where companies increasingly focus on introducing AI to nearly every level of their business. In fact, the AI-first mindset will transform many industries.

We are racing towards a world of hyper-personalization, known in marketing as the segment of one (or audience of one). Spammy mass marketing is no longer acceptable, and such strategies will not be efficient going forward. With inbound content marketing becoming the norm, so are highly personalized customer experiences, with individualized marketing touch-points, where the right person gets the right message, in the right channel, at the right time.

One can argue that AI will make marketing relevant again. For decades, the friendly and familiar corner shop of the past was replaced by mass media that lacked personalization or an understanding of each person's context and needs. AI can enable us to place the customer in the center again and give personalized experiences throughout the customer journey. We can turn mass-marketing into a personal conversation, like the corner store of old. The difference today is that it is automated and done at unprecedented scale.

AI will also make marketing more efficient and cost effective. Using machine learning algorithms, we can deploy self-learning systems that know how to optimize themselves to become continually better. Optimize what? Almost everything. Here are just a few examples:

- Email send times, cadence, and subject lines that give the highest open-rates
- Blog content that gives the highest engagement and SEO performance
- Predictions about which leads are more likely to convert into customers

- The most relevant product search results and product recommendations
- Social media analytics, posting, or moderation
- Business and competitor intelligence
- Ad purchase and campaign optimization
- The entire customer journey

There are even AI-tools that generate website designs automatically. Other tools can perform conversion ratio optimization, complete with automated design changes proposed, implemented, and tested by genetic algorithms. Unless you have studied the field of AI-driven marketing before, you will likely be shocked to learn what can be automated using machine learning today. Here, we give just an appetizer of the feast to come.

We are entering a world where marketing decisions are based on billions or trillions of data points, easily outperforming the gut feeling of any skilled marketer. Marketing will not only be data-driven and fact-based, it will learn over time and optimize its own behavior. In other words, marketing systems will adjust automatically to changing customer behavior or other external factors. This raises an interesting question: Will marketers have a job in five years? If so, what will that job look like? We'll talk more about this in the chapters to come.

Key Terms

Before we get to the main topic, let's cover a crash course in what AI is and how it works. While some readers will already know this, it's best to have a firm footing before going into more detail. This section is the mile high overview.

Three main technologies have together enabled artificial intelligence: big-data, predictive analytics, and machine learning. But what are they?

Big data means the collection and analysis of huge collections of information—sometimes trillions of pieces. When examined properly, this enables the detection of almost invisible trends and correlations. We can, for example, detect patterns in historical data that correlate to certain types of credit card transactions being fraudulent. Predictive analytics is about designing algorithms that can detect these patterns in future unknown data. For example, to detect if a current credit card transaction fits such patterns, and then determine if the transaction is likely fraudulent.

Machine learning refers to predictive analytics algorithms that can adapt to changing environmental conditions. These software solutions retrain themselves and learn to make even better predictions in the future. In effect, they become self-optimizing, or self-learning. Predictive systems can only detect anomalies based on the patterns on which they were originally trained; if something changes in their environment, they are unable to adapt. With machine learning, the prediction system is continually retrained to make different predictions when new data become available based on the latest types of fraud from the real world.

Think of it this way: With machine learning, the software behavior is based on historical data. This process is called "training" the system. If new data becomes available later, we can retrain the system to make it adapt its behavior to changing conditions. When a prediction system is retrained often (or even continuously), it continues to adapt its predictions to reflect changes in the outside world. Thus, while they may seem like magic, predictive and machine learning systems are driven by collected, real-world data.

Predictive machine learning algorithms are commonly classified by how they learn. The three main types of learning are supervised, unsupervised, and reinforcement. What's the difference?

- Supervised learning: the algorithms are trained to do a particular task using historical data.
- Unsupervised learning: insights are found using historical data, even if we don't know exactly what we are looking for.
- Reinforcement learning: the algorithms are trained by positive or negative experiences, or in other words, using trial and error.

Similarly, AI algorithms are often classified by what they do:

- Classification algorithms predict one of several possibilities, e.g. to determine if a customer is likely to buy a specific product or not.

- Regression algorithms predict a numeric value in any range, e.g. to determine the best price of a product.
- Clustering algorithms predict group similarity, e.g. to find segments of your leads and customers with similar attributes.

AI-tools are often used in marketing to process natural language. So far, we have seen software that can react to certain keywords and phrases, but increasingly, AI is able to understand normal spoken language, with all its idiosyncrasies and variations. In fact, I'd argue language processing is overrepresented in marketing tools compared to other uses of AI, such as in manufacturing, maintenance, or logistics. Tools that can understand and mimic natural speech are used in a wide range of marketing tasks, including competitor intelligence, social media analysis, chatbots, email subject line optimization, content marketing, and even website domain name pricing. An entire subfield of AI is dedicated to text processing, and you may want to be familiar with these terms:

- Natural Language Processing (NLP) is about processing text. This can be to check its grammar or conduct some analysis that doesn't require an understanding of the writer's intent.
- Natural Language Understanding (NLU) builds upon NLP and is about comprehending the actual meaning of a text, for example to know that an email is about booking a meeting or a price request for a particular service, even taking the current context of the conversation into account.
- Natural Language Generation (NLG) is about creating human-sounding text, sometimes in response to incoming text understood by NLU.

With this type of language tool, AI is moving beyond just being behind the scenes and is now interacting directly with people. Sometimes, you may not even know you are dealing with a robot. We are increasingly able to avoid what AI researchers call the uncanny valley—that strange feeling you get when an AI is *almost* right, but lacks an intangible level of humanity. In the coming years, the bar will continue to be raised for how well computers mimic and are perceived to be human.

The topic of AI development also creates media hype and a certain level of fear mongering about the risks of run-away machines, as we've seen in movies ranging from *2001: A Space Odyssey* to *The Minority Report*. Hollywood can give us alarming ideas as to what artificial intelligence currently is. To clarify this, let's look at the true scope of AI so we can put the hype and these sci-fi predictions in context.

Myths and Misconceptions

When we talk about AI, for the most part, we don't mean real artificial intelligence like we see in the movies. In most cases, we mean machine learning, or perhaps predictive analytics. Essentially, this is just a clever use of statistics. Artificial intelligence is broken into two categories: 'Weak' or 'narrow' AI, and 'strong' or 'general' AI.

- Weak AI generally refers to a machine learning solution dedicated to one specific task only, such as optimizing the price of a product or the send time of an email. This is not real intelligence, just statistical algorithms that can adapt their behavior as the data they are trained on changes.
- Strong AI, on the other hand, is a flexible and general-purpose system that can think and reason on its own, solving problems it hasn't been trained to do in advance. Perhaps they could become aware of their own existence too, just like a human being.

Only weak AI exists today, and everything discussed in this book is on that side of the divide. That doesn't mean these systems are less effective in performing their tasks; on the contrary, they can be incredibly impressive, as we will discover. However, you don't need to worry about marketing AI systems taking over the world—at least not for now. However, even weak AI can still cause problems, such as affecting the outcome of public elections, as we learned through the scandal of Cambridge Analytica and its role in the 2016 US election.

For the remainder of this book, we will look only at weak AI solutions that offer self-learning algorithms to solve specific problems for which they have been developed. I also use the terms 'AI' and 'machine learning' interchangeably.

Chapter Summary

In this chapter, we introduced artificial intelligence in the context of marketing, explained some of the most important terms, and covered the difference between strong and weak AI. Later chapters will dive deeper into how AI works in greater detail and explain how you can develop your own machine learning solutions to improve the competitiveness of your company. We will also explain what new technologies are waiting around the corner.

Before we go that far, it is important to understand how you can leverage AI by simply purchasing pre-built marketing products that build or improve their capabilities thanks to this revolutionary technology. With existing tools on the market, you can leverage the benefits of predictive marketing and machine-learning without the need to know how they work. Let's look at what current marketing tools can already do using AI, and how to pick the ones that are best for your company.

HOW DOES MARKETING SOFTWARE USE AI?

Business and marketing managers may not know where to start on their journey towards an AI-powered future. In this chapter, we will work through an overview of what existing commercial solutions can already do to help in marketing and running a business with AI. We'll look at a range of common needs and how specific products can address them.

It's important to note that while many vendors are mentioned by name here, that does not imply a personal endorsement. However, I am pleased to feature some of the leading or otherwise interesting companies in the industry. With that said, there are more to be explored and leveraged, and the landscape changes almost daily. Additionally, I want to mention that I am not affiliated with any of the vendors mentioned, and receive no payment from them, financial or otherwise. Now, let's look at the landscape of AI systems available today.

Giving Your Company an Edge

This chapter looks at how AI-powered software can help address some common marketing and business problems. These include market and competitive intelligence, pricing, e-commerce and ad optimization, and more. First, we'll discuss how AI can increase competitive intelligence, giving you insights into what is happening on the market beyond what is accessible by human researchers. We then move on to more specific tasks, such as predictive pricing and ad strategy optimization.

Competitive Intelligence

Getting market insights and an understanding of what your competitors are doing can be a major advantage. Companies have performed market analysis and competitive intelligence for decades, trying to make sense of their external environment, but the landscape is changing dramatically now. The reason, of course, is that the Internet—combined with advanced data analytics and AI—can provide so much more information on what others in your field are doing.

With more and more business activities moving online, with most of their activities in plain sight, it has never been easier to gather competitor intelligence. Every company that is reasonably active online will leave digital footprints that are open for anyone to watch and interpret. If they don't, their customers, employees, and partners do. At the same time, this creates vast amounts of information, making it hard to digest manually. In practice, it is almost impossible to keep up.

The process of gathering and analyzing market and competitive intelligence clearly benefits from having the right tools, and artificial intelligence is well positioned to help. What can AI tools for competitive intelligence do? In short, they help gather data and turn them into strategic insights you can use as part of your strategies. You can spy on competitors and their products, obviously, but also partners, industry influencers, customers, review or career sites, or other organizations related to your market. Any information about your industry and those involved in it can be gathered and analyzed at unprecedented scales.

Competitor websites are a prime location to study, including product description pages or press releases on websites and in the news. Companies often publish information on new customers or new partnerships, events they will attend, financial updates, news on acquisitions, and more. Monitoring this can be rewarding.

Any publicly advertised or announced hiring, downsizing, or management team changes can provide valuable insights as well. If they hire, what positions are they filling and in which local office? Are they opening or closing any offices? Have they replaced their CFO or a business unit manager? Data like this may signal areas where they are investing or are dealing with problems. The most obvious thing to monitor may be the competitors' product pages. There is often a lot to learn about product improvements, positioning, and market message, as well as pricing and insights into the general business model.

You may also benefit from collecting customer reviews from competing products, product review sites, or product forums. Many companies publish customer success stories and testimonials, or highlight new partnerships. Finally, social media channels, blogs, and scheduled webinars may provide a wealth of information on what products or marketing resources your competitors promote, what customers say about them, and more.

It's nearly impossible to monitor this type of information manually for all your competitors and other organizations relevant to your industry, and even harder to generate meaningful insights from it. Tool support is clearly needed, and there are many options to choose from. Some of these tools can provide near real-time insights as well. To make sense of the information gathered online, most of these tools use natural language processing (NLP) and natural language understanding (NLU) to harvest business insights from text.

Crayon, for example, claims to follow over a hundred different types of signals for each of your competitors. Their system collects information from millions of data sources and uses machine learning to improve the results. Their tool tracks your competitor's digital footprint both on and off their websites, thus detecting their activities and what is said about them online. This may range from product and price changes to customer and employee reviews or marketing campaigns. In essence, it is a digital analyst tracking a competitor's moves, automatically and at scale. For example, if a competitor launches a product that is immediately met by criticisms about its suitability or functionality, these systems can provide the necessary data to create your own product free of those drawbacks, thus offering consumers a more attractive alternative.

I discussed their tool with Ellie Mirman, CMO at Crayon. She mentions that often, the most critical updates are those that aren't announced in press releases, but rather are hidden in subtle website changes or a new customer review. She is probably right, but sifting through so much detailed data on a regular basis is just not possible to do manually. This needs to be addressed by software automation.

Mirman notes, "With the incredible amount of intelligence data available, it's critical to surface the highest priority updates to be able to analyze and act on them while they are still fresh. Crayon uses a combination of machine learning and analyst curation to separate the signal from the noise in competitive intelligence." Given the volumes of data, the latter may be both important and difficult to solve using traditional software technologies. By leveraging AI, the system is able to tell the difference between the correction of a typo on a homepage (not mean-ingful) versus the change of one number on a pricing page (meaningful).

Harvesting valuable insights from vast amounts of data is indeed one of the best use-cases of artificial intelligence, and is becoming one of the most common. Another vendor in this space is Quid, which can analyze markets and brand perception. Quid discovers patterns and trends, and monitors what customers say in conversations about a company, their products, or the wider market.

While some of the information these systems use could have been gathered by pre-existing content scraping tools, artificial intelligence tools are able to understand the meaning and content of the information they find, turning data into actionable insights. This is a big difference. With AI, we not only get help in gathering the data from a huge number of sources, it can also understand what is written and condense the infor-mation into the most important insights.

Predictive Pricing

Setting the right price is a key factor in business success. Still, many com-panies use gut feeling rather than facts when determining the cost of their products. With predictive pricing, we can apply machine learning to the problem of setting the best price and improve revenue optimization. We can change the price dynamically too. Dynamic pricing is often divided into two categories: revenue management, which is driven by supply like hotel rooms or seats on a flight, and supply driven, which is propelled by competitor price-matching or out-of-stocks.

Customer acceptance for dynamic pricing is generally quite high for products with fluctuating availability and demand, where the product by nature vanishes after a certain time. Take a global car rental company with thousands of locations as an example. They may change millions of prices each day to optimize their revenue based on a huge number of fac-tors, from the weather, to local events, to the prices of their competitors. This can clearly not be done manually, and prediction algorithms can help find the optimal pricing for each car, in each location, at every hour.

Luckily, readymade solutions for revenue optimization exist, and they can predict the best price of most products—provided you have enough data to crunch. One example is Perfect Price, which offers a product that covers both revenue management and supply-driven situations. I had a conversation with Alexander Shartsis, co-founder and CEO of Perfect Price. He says that "Today, consumers accept and even expect price fluctuations. Frequently, they are able to time them better than the companies setting the prices—costing companies billions annually. It seemed clear that there should be a simple service to automate the complex data science required to make dynamic pricing possible for any business."

Perfect Price leverages a core platform based on a number of AI technologies, including supervised machine learning, reinforcement learning, clustering, and more. This platform generates a demand function that is accurate down to the micro-segment level, meaning it is specific for very small groups of customers. It then can calculate an optimal price based on business rules and other configurable parameters in order to optimize the customer's objective—profit, revenue, etc.

It is obvious this type of technology can benefit many companies, in particular those where the pricing is changing often, as is the case with flight tickets, rental cars, and hotel rooms. Additionally, AI can be used to predict the most likely selling price for certain goods that are never exactly the same, like the price of a used car or a house on the real-estate market.

In such cases, data about the sale of similar products are gathered over time, for example the selling price of used cars, along with data attributes like the type of engine, stereo, color, mileage, equipment, the owner's neighborhood, and more. Given this data, a price prediction algorithm can guess the most likely selling price for the next used car to be sold, even though it has never seen exactly the same combination of attributes before. This works similarly for real estate properties and other categories of products where there is only one unit of the same configuration available. Regression algorithms are suitable for this kind of functionality, and we'll look at them in more detail later.

An unexpected example of a solution like this comes from GoDaddy, the web hosting and domain name supplier. Their domain value and appraisal tool uses natural language processing to understand the word combinations used in a domain name. It then predicts the price of the domains using those words on the domain name aftermarket. That's why when you go to buy a domain, the one you want may be expensive, while similar ones without the same pull can be quite cheap.

Ads Strategy

Many companies invest large sums on digital advertisements, and AI is well-positioned to optimize ad investments. In particular, machine learning can be used in optimization of programmatic display ads. For example, AppNexus and PulsePoint both provide programmatic ad solutions, offering ad purchasing and sales based on machine learning. Other tools analyze ad spending and results across channels; not only your own, but also that of your competitors. This is ad intelligence for the benefit of both buyers and sellers.

The digital advertising ecosystem is complex and changes quickly. Advertisers have a difficult time getting transparency on their own ads, not to mention what their competitors are doing. Many layers prevent transparency, especially in the programmatic markets, where an ad impression can pass through a number of providers—from publisher to advertiser—before being filled. Having insight into which advertisers are buying on which publisher sites and through which networks and exchanges helps everyone make better decisions.

Pathmatics is a company in this space that offers what can be described as a search engine for ads. They use machine learning to gather insights into ad spending and impressions, which can help companies respond to competitor activities or improve results in future campaigns. I had a conversation with Kenneth Roberts, Head of Marketing at Pathmatics. He explained:

> *For buyers of advertising—brands and their agencies—timely information on their competitors' advertising can make a major impact on the effectiveness of their own marketing and advertising performance. A brand, for example, can know if a competitor has launched a new marketing campaign or started spending for impressions on a new site (potentially a new target market). The brand marketers can compare themselves within their category and determine if they are being outspent. Advertisers can find sites that they are not advertising on—and the most efficient channel partner to*

buy through. They can also monitor brand safety and detect wasteful placements to cut or reallocate spend.

Pathmatics and similar companies can report on information such as desktop display, pre-roll video, mobile web, native, and social advertising. For example, the Pathmatics pipeline for detecting ads, estimating impressions, and calculating potential spending uses machine learning models that are constantly updated with market data on prices, ad formats, site traffic, and indexed digital ad data.

It is easy to see how ad intelligence can be a marketing advantage over your competitors. You can even let AI-based software automation tools manage and optimize campaigns autonomously—from purchasing ads to analyzing results. In essence, you can get a virtual digital marketer that manages and executes self-driven and self-optimizing digital marketing campaigns.

This is exactly what Albert Technologies does. You provide the creatives and goals, and their software tool (an AI agent they call Albert) uses machine learning to initiate and optimize ad spending across different media channels and devices over time. It measures the results and adapts the ad investments automatically as the ROI changes.

Or Shani, the CEO and founder of Albert Technologies explains, "Albert is autonomous, or self-driven, meaning that he can create digital marketing interactions unassisted, using the results of multivariate tests and deep-level analysis to make better decisions moving forward." He also notes, "Albert can run thousands and thousands of tests across hundreds and hundreds of variables in a very brief window of time."

Whereas traditional solutions simply analyze data and then wait for a human to make a decision about it, AI tools like Albert can analyze the data, determine the best course of action, execute it, and then continually optimize itself in real time based on what it learns.

While Pathmatics and Albert are general tools for working on multiple channels, you may want to consider specific platforms only as well. If you are interested in Google Adwords more specifically, AdScale offers algorithmic bid and budget management based on machine learning to help optimize advertising performance. StrikeSocial does something similar, but on YouTube.

It's one thing to optimize the campaign at large, but another to optimize the ad creative itself. Dynamic creative optimization is the process of adapting the creative to the person seeing it in real time. A huge amount of data can be mined to predict which creative will trigger someone to convert. Some tools address ad optimization from this angle, for example by predicting the creative quality of your different ads, the optimal number of ads you should use simultaneously, and the best creative refresh cadence to avoid ad fatigue. Have a look at Refuel4 or Spongecell if you are interested in this. Additionally, Adobe is now starting to add AI capabilities to Photoshop and their marketing cloud products as well. More and more specialized tools are becoming available, which promises an interesting future for marketers. Only time will tell how much AI will be able to automate graphic design in the future.

E-commerce and Omni-channel

AI and machine learning can be used in nearly every stage of the customer journey for e-commerce businesses; for example, auto-generation of product descriptions, predictive pricing and personalization of product searches, product recommendations, and other types of content. Email marketing and customer service can be improved, and even virtual shopping bots that integrate into the e-commerce solution are available. In effect, the experience becomes customer-centric and hyper-personalized.

In a data-driven world, companies already have demographic, behavioral, and transactional data at their disposal, but they are often missing information regarding the motivation and personality of their shoppers. By analyzing shoppers' behavior (e.g., click-through, add-to-cart, and check out data) in response to specific persuasive messaging, it is possible to collect psychographic data that explains the psychological tendencies of individuals.

This is what Crobox does. In essence, they bring AI-powered behavioral psychology to e-commerce. Janelle de Weerd, Marketing Manager at Crobox explains that their products help e-commerce companies discover the *why* behind the *buy* with the delivery of unique psychographic data that boosts business performance. Their solution tries to find the best products to highlight with persuasive triggers. Then, after uncovering the optimal products, it matches the best persuasive message to that product.

This is similar to conversion ratio optimization, with a layer of psychology added to it. I am no psychologist, but Weerd's elaboration made it clearer to me: "Based on the findings discovered through our experimentation, we provide our clients with in-depth reports about their shoppers' psychographic profiles. This gives our clients more clarity on the subconscious motivations of their shoppers and actionable insight into what persuasion tactics work best in triggering online behavior."

Other e-commerce specific features include up-selling and cross-selling, abandoned shopping cart management, discount coupons, etc. Traditionally, this has often been driven by RFM (recency, frequency, and monetary value) analysis. Many e-commerce businesses are unaware of what possibilities are now available to them, and the early adopters will see an advantage over the laggards. It will be interesting to see how fast this type of technology comes into widespread use.

Nowadays, a much more holistic view can be analyzed using integrated customer data platforms and machine learning algorithms. It is now possible to get much better insights, for example using calculations such as customer lifetime value (CLTV), customer acquisition cost (CAC), churn prediction, and retention by value segment. Lead scoring and audience management can further help find the right types of customers. For larger organizations, in particular those with physical stores as well, customer data platforms (CDPs) with support for retail and omni-channel businesses may be a better fit. Examples include AgilOne, CaliberMind, Ometria, and Zylotech.

Ivan Mazour, CEO and Founder of retail-focused Ometria, summarizes his company as "a customer marketing platform that helps retailers better understand, and better communicate with their customers."

To do this, they connect the touchpoints customers have had with your business by integrating the key ERP, retail, marketing, and e-commerce platforms. They then import and aggregate those touchpoints. Mazour adds, "Our intelligence layer then runs in real-time across all of these profiles to identify their interests, as well as appropriate actions to take, and appropriate times to take these actions."

One example of how they use AI for this is in predicting when a customer may be at risk of never buying again. Typically in retail, this is done on a rules basis: if they haven't shopped in twelve months, they're at risk. Ometria uses AI to calculate a predictive at-risk score, on an individual basis for each customer, based on all of their interactions—buying, visiting the website, and so on. This improves relevancy and accuracy, and of course, the marketing ROI.

Systems like this leverage the insights made by starting personalized and context-specific marketing activities, perhaps by sending personalized marketing emails offering the product the system thinks this customer is most likely to by next. With companies like Ometria, churn prediction is a common feature in these systems, and automated marketing outreach can be initiated to prevent customers from defecting.

A company called OrderGroove takes a somewhat different route and promotes a solution for relationship commerce and predictive re-ordering. They simplify customer ordering and re-ordering for omni-channel companies with a solution that prompts existing customers to purchase the same product again at the time prediction algorithms determine is right. This comes through a simple response on SMS or email, or by using subscription plans. Functionalities for automated predictive re-ordering may be of particular interest to companies offering replenishment products. All-in-all, we can expect various types of AI-powered functionalities to improve e-commerce and become more of a widely used commodity in the years to come.

Business Anomaly Detection

With the vast amounts of data being produced in businesses today, there is no way for humans to sift through all of it to stay ahead. Relying on manual monitoring means important insights are missed often. It would be nice to have a tool that monitors all of your business data and notifies you automatically when unexpected changes happen in customer behavior, demographics, and conversions.

A tool addressing this problem is Outlier.ai, which takes a new approach to business intelligence. Instead of creating new dashboards and running queries when questions arise, Outlier solves this problem by sending an email each morning with the top few anomalies going on in the business. By tailoring insights to each individual staff member, it is like giving everyone at your company a dedicated business analyst who is constantly looking for hidden problems and opportunities.

Sean Byrnes is the CEO and founder of Outlier.ai. He shares an interesting insight from his former career, which led him to start the new company: "I met with hundreds of companies to discuss how they use data to make decisions. The most common question they would ask me is 'What should I look for in all of this data I have?' I realized that the last ten years of business intelligence innovation had centered on answering questions we already had, while the next ten years would focus on helping us ask better questions."

This captures the ideal use of AI: moving from drowning in historical data to being served with the right insights automatically. To offer this capability, Outlier and similar emerging platforms use different machine-learning algorithms that turn raw data into human-readable insights, understand what is normal, detect anomalous events, and filter through the clusters of events to select the few that best match the interests of each user. Expect most business intelligence tools to be AI-powered in the future.

Contracts and Legal Agreements

While not strictly part of marketing, reviewing and signing contracts and legal agreements are common tasks in management and business. Clearly, many people find it both intimidating and boring to study the legalese in such documents. Can AI help? As you may assume by now, the answer is a resounding yes.

Several AI tools specialize in helping both non-lawyers and professional attorneys understand complex contracts and legalese for contract and license analysis, as well as document compliance and research into legal matters. Have a look at Beagle, Casetext, Luminance, or LegalRobot if you want to use virtual lawyers in your business.

Content Marketing

Content marketing is all the rage these days, as the Content Marketing Institute and MarketingProfs notes in their 2018 B2B Content Marketing report.[9] A full 91% of American B2B businesses use content market-ing, according to the report, which is an 18% increase compared to the year before. Still, only 9% of the companies perform content marketing strategy, and only 11% measure the result of their content marketing efforts. These are areas where AI can help marketers.

Marketing guru Seth Godin has claimed that "content marketing is the only marketing left." This is why many companies are compet-ing with each other to fill the Internet with content that help improve their organic reach (search engine optimization), build their authority and thought leadership, and increase engagement. This has largely led to what is called the content shock, in which the Internet is flooded with content, thus overwhelming leads and customers. Additionally, it is in-creasingly becoming a costly burden to keep producing all the content to stay ahead of competition. Can AI help here? As it turns out, yes. Thanks to natural language processing (NLP), understanding (NLU), and gener-ation (NLG), tools can not only understand natural language, but gen-erate human-sounding text too. This is a pre-requisite for software-based content marketing. Let's look at a few aspects of content marketing and how AI will continue to change the game.

Content Strategy

Content strategy is about measuring what content provides a meaningful ROI and marketing value, enabling content managers to double-down on producing content that generates leads and customers, and scale back on content that doesn't provide good results. Search engines like Google are now focused on providing search results of high quality. Their search algorithms are becoming good at finding high quality content, and it is becoming increasingly hard to trick them (this is called black hat SEO).

To this end, content strategy tools have started to emerge. For ex-ample, HubSpot measures domain and page authority (these are SEO metrics) and use artificial intelligence to recommend topics on which to produce content. They promote the concept of content clusters, where supporting content (often a number of blog posts) links to a piece of

9   "B2B Content Marketing," Content Marketing Institute, 2018. *https://contentmarket-inginstitute.com/wp-content/uploads/2017/09/2018_B2B_Research_FINAL.pdf*

long-form pillar content to help push its authority in the eyes of search engines.

AI and machine learning can be used to help improve the quality of the content as well, either for better SEO ranking or to provide readers with exactly the content they are looking for (and are thus more likely to engage with). Software tools can use AI to model a topic and build content briefs that show exactly how to write to systematically cover a topic in the best way. For example, what are the relevant concepts to mention in the content? What are the questions to answer? How should content be written to make it rank in search engines?

One company offering a solution for this is MarketMuse. Their tool enables the creation of better articles, increases topic coverage across a website, observes and analyzes the competitive landscape, and discovers content improvement priorities. I discussed their tool with Aki Balogh, the company's co-founder and CEO. He describes his product in this way:

"By using the MarketMuse methodology, marketers can build more comprehensive content and establish authority on topics relevant to their business, resulting in enhanced organic website traffic, improved thought leadership and improved rates of customer conversion."

MarketMuse is interesting because it scours massive amounts of web content to look for the coverage around a focus topic. It builds a topic model that helps a marketer write like a subject matter expert. This enables the creation of high-quality content that ranks in search engines. In effect, the platform helps connect the dots between what the content marketers want to write about and what the users want to know. This helps improve engagement, increases search rankings, and develops thought leadership.

Large corporations with many employees can have different problems, including adhering to a consistent voice or brand guidelines. By now, it may come as no surprise to learn that AI can gather brand and audience goals and help ensure your content complies with those goals. After all, most corporations want to give a consistent message.

Such tools use AI for content scoring and brand compliance checking, enabling all different pieces of content to be coherent across offices or content producers. Other content strategy tools help with auditing your content, understanding how people behave in relation to your content, benchmarking your competitors' content, and generating data-driven content ideas. Some content strategy tools optimize what and how you should write, as well as where and when it should be published for the best return on investment. Several tools on the market address such problems, for example Acrolinx, BrightEdge, Concured, and Atomic Reach.

Content Creation

As AI solutions not only analyze and understand text, but generate human-sounding text too, there are many use-cases in content creation. Let's start with AI-assisted manual content creation. A great use of AI in content creation is advanced grammar checking. Since I am Swedish, English is my second language. While Microsoft Word or Apple Pages have built-in spell checkers with grammar control, they aren't best-in-class and I could do with some more help.

I have thus used a stand-alone grammar checker for years. It is called Grammarly and uses machine learning to improve its grammar checking over time. In fact, this area is so hot that they raised over $100 million USD in venture capital in 2017 to improve their product even further. Grammarly is an AI-based natural language processing tool (NLP) that processes and analyses the copy you have written and recommends improvements.

Another interesting area is natural language generation. NLG tools doesn't read and analyze your content, they write it. While it may sound like science fiction, already several tools can do this. One of them is Wordsmith from Automated Insights. Their tool converts structured data (say, information in an Excel spreadsheet or a database) into natural language text. They claim to generate 1.5 billion pieces of narrative content each year for customers like Microsoft, Cisco, the Associated Press, Yahoo, PwC, and more.

Wordsmith can be used to write product descriptions in e-commerce, property listings for real estate agencies, stock market portfolio descriptions in the financial industry, and similar documents for practically any other industry. It can also be used to generate data-driven and highly personalized email copy. In effect, Wordsmith can generate unique copy from the inputted data. Think robot journalism here.

If you are an e-commerce company and want to upload 1250 product descriptions to your web shop, you can feed the raw product data from an Excel spreadsheet into Wordsmith. The software will then auto-generate 1250 engaging product descriptions in a matter of seconds. The Wordsmith team has extended the usability of their writing robot with an API (an application programming interface), thus enabling external software solutions to integrate with it to produce fully automated text generation solutions for your company's needs.

Narrative Science is a similar company, with an NLG product called Quill. It too transforms raw structured data into natural language narratives using artificial intelligence and machine learning. Their NLG engine is designed to produce human-like, intuitive language. It automatically utilizes variable word choice, understands when it's best to combine sentences, and identifies the appropriate pronoun usage, verb tense, and grammar to produce fluid, conversational language that is easily consumable. This is how Aimee Rowland, Director of Product Marketing at Narrative Science, explains their product:

"Our technology not only utilizes NLG to generate natural language explanations, but it also utilizes a range of analytical, reasoning, and learning capabilities to identify the most interesting and important insights, all with domain-specific knowledge so that it understands the context behind the data."

Their technology highlights the most interesting and important facts from data, providing relevant insights for each intended audience. It does this by performing context-aware analysis focused on the core of what needs to be communicated. After all, it is not only about generating text, it is also important that it covers the right information.

Both Automated Insights and Narrative Science offer report generators that turn Google Analytics web usage data into insightful narrative reports. This can be a great aid to marketers who need to write management reports.

The news media is also turning to AI and NLG for automatic generation of articles. The Washington Post, for example, uses their own in-house AI robot for article creation. It is called Heliograph and is said to have produced 850 articles in the last year, including many relating to sports.[10]

Many local newspapers, even relatively small ones, already use robot journalism to turn numeric data into articles. Short articles on local sports results are prime examples here, as are weather reports, traffic information, and police blotters.

Now, content marketing and content production can be automated at scale. Don't see it as a replacement of your copywriter, but an opportunity to automate parts of the content production efforts, in particular areas where massive amounts of data just couldn't be converted into natural language text due to the time and cost required. Add to this the possibilities for hyper-personalization, where each customer gets different content based on the data you have on them.

Other interesting tools include ArticleForge, Articoolo and AI-Writer. With these, you simply type a phrase in an edit field—for example, "car insurance". The tools then harvest the internet for relevant information, and return an auto-generated article on that topic, of your desired word length. At least one of these tools can even auto-generate hundreds of different variations in one go, enabling you to publish many similar articles that use completely different text. While the results may vary with different tools, they are getting better each day and can act as a quick-start that you refine further. Beware of copyright infringements, though, if you use phrases from other people's websites.

Did you know AI tools can auto-generate videos? They can, at least semi-automatically. I've used Lumen5 for a while and I find it simple to use. This innovative tool aims to automate the process of creating short videos, in particular for promoting blog posts on social media using video clips of a minute or two.

Feed it with the URL of the blog post, and it finds what it thinks is the most relevant captions to use as headings. It then lay out the headings on scenes (similar to PowerPoint pages) and uses AI to find free images and video clips on the Internet that relate to the keywords in the selected headings. At the end, it adds animated scene transitions, allows

---

10   For a sample article, see "Wilson at Yorktown," *The Washington Post*, 31 August 2017. *https://www.washingtonpost.com/allmetsports/2017-fall/games/football/87055/*

you to select music, and exports a video into standard file formats. You can transform text into video in minutes, even if you do some manual editing of the preselected options. This is pretty amazing and a clear sign of where we are heading. I can't wait to see what tools like this can do in five or ten years.

Content Curation

Content curation is about finding high-quality relevant content from external sources and promoting it to help build your authority and engagement. Similar to content creation, curation can be automated using AI and machine learning. With this type of tool, you can engage in data-driven content marketing at scale with a minimum of effort. I'm sure you'd like to generate more and better marketing content in less time. Who wouldn't?

Curata and Scoop.it can help with that. They aim to find and curate content, and then help to distribute it, measuring the results at the same time. They find the most relevant and popular content for your company's customer base and improve the marketing results from your investment in content publishing.

Take Hawkeye from Scoop.it as an example. This content intelligence platform enables marketers to analyze and measure web content. It eliminates the guesswork in content marketing by providing data-driven insights to marketers that help them define their content strategy, create better content, identify influencers to work with, and measure their content performance against competitors.

When talking with Guillaume Decugis, Co-Founder and CEO of Scoop.it, he explained, "Hawkeye indexes the web's editorial content from mainstream media sites to niche industry blogs. By using a unique combination of data sources—including content sources provided by the Scoop.it community of more than four million users—Hawkeye has access to content from tens of millions of sources over the world in any language."

Each piece of content is then measured, and its quality is scored and performance assessed. Marketers can query Hawkeye's database to better understand their content universe. In particular, they can identify top-performing content and influencers on that topic, analyze their competitors' content to identify what topics they've been successful with, and identify trending topics that are getting traction.

Another company, Vestorly, enables personalized, news-driven content marketing curated by artificial intelligence. Their tool scans and indexes the Internet for relevant content to curate, determines the interests of all the individual contacts in your database by harvesting their social media engagement and other online activities, and choses individualized curated content for each contact in your audience.

The tool then sends or publishes the personalized curated content in the form of newsletter emails, social media posts, or dynamic content streamed as a content feed to your website. In effect, each person in your audience gets content recommendations that are most engaging for their particular interests.

Justin Wisz, CEO of Vestorly, says that this "enables users to scale authentic engagement (with an average 300% lift in email engagement rates) while reducing marketing tasks, leading to stronger client relationships, increased referrals, and lead generation."

I find it interesting to see AI not just helping with content curation, but personalizing it for each individual contact based on their personal interests. No marketer or organization would have the time to do this manually for anything but audiences of trivial sizes. This is a great example of how AI can extend a marketing team's capabilities into areas they realistically couldn't handle before.

Content Repurposing

With the rising popularity of podcast audio shows and video, it would be nice to get an automatic transcription into text that can then be published as a blog post. While search engines surely will be able to search in audio and video soon, to my knowledge, search results are still mostly based on text. I expect this to change shortly, but for now you may need to convert your audio podcast or YouTube videos into text for search engines like Google to index them. Turning audio into text is a tedious and labor-intensive task that would benefit from automation.

Tools for this exist, for example Trint or Nuance's Dragon. Even YouTube can now create subtitles from the audio stream automatically. The required voice understanding is all based on AI algorithms, of course, but AI tools can do a lot of useful stuff for text repurposing too.

Articoolo and WordAI can rewrite any text into a completely different text with the same meaning (paraphrasing). This could help repurpose old blog posts into e-books with similar text that doesn't appear to be the same, for example. This also creates the risk of massive copying of other people's content, with automatic repurposing to make it look unique. I am no legal advisor, but how would copyright law apply to completely new text that is auto-generated from other people's copyrighted content? Like many of the tools we are looking at here, the legal and ethical considerations are substantial. We'll look at this in more detail later.

Report Generation

Report generation is closely related to content creation, but I see the latter more as robot journalism or copywriting for external use, whereas report generation is a mechanical process of repetitively generating narrated reports from raw data, say monthly sales reports or website traffic reports.

PaveAI is an example of a report generation tool. They take raw Google Analytics data of website user behavior and turn it into a text-based report in natural language with noticeable insights detected and presented automatically. You can create your own AI-driven insightful reports covering other data as well, thus automating tedious work preparing recurring reports for internal use or for distribution to your customers.

Public Speaking

Running seminars and other types of public speeches are common tasks for many business leaders and product marketers. I've made many public speeches myself over the past two decades of my career.

I remember one of my first speeches. It was in Chicago, which in itself was intimidating for a then twenty-something newly employed software engineer from Sweden. The speech went surprisingly well, and I even received a review score well above the average of veteran American speakers, which wasn't too bad considering my somewhat poor English and lack of experience. This was a great advantage, as it gave me the confidence to do it again.

I was fortunate enough to continue my career with interesting trips to exotic countries to make many public speeches in the following two decades. I traveled to countries like Japan, South Korea, Taiwan, and many places in Europe and North America. The most memorable—in a negative way—was a speech I made in Korea in front of 250 or so engineers who didn't understand English. I had a translator helping me translate to Korean, but sadly, she was shocked by the microphone on stage and fell to the floor looking rather dead. Fortunately, she wasn't seriously hurt, but I had to continue the speech on my own, in front of an audience that probably didn't understand much of what I said. I didn't receive a performance score that time, but it likely wouldn't have been positive.

The moral of the story? Being a speaker isn't always easy, and unexpected events may alter the quality of your performance. With that said, event organizers would benefit from quality scoring of public speakers, and speakers would appreciate help in improving their speaking skills. So, what does this have to do with AI?

Believe it or not, there are AI solutions that help improve public speeches. A company called Gweekspeech offers speech intelligence solutions, helping public speakers benchmark and improve their performances. Their product uses cognitive technology that performs speech intelligence on communication and presentation skills, thus helping to improve oratory and public speech skills. This is probably one of the more unexpected uses of AI in marketing I have come across so far, but certainly an interesting one.

Additionally, content strategy tools like MarketMuse can be used to understand what topics and keywords to include in a presentation to cover a topic as completely as possible—at least as it appears from harvesting data on the topic from the Internet.

Lead and Customer Acquisition

Machine learning can be used in many ways to help acquire more leads and customers. In this section, we will look at some of them, including ways to find new prospects, manage conversion optimization, and conduct attribution modeling to help optimize the ROI of your marketing investments.

Sales Prospecting

All companies lose some customers sooner or later, and to survive, it is crucial to get new ones. With enough new customers, you will not only maintain the business, but grow as well. AI can have several applications here. For example, it can be used to recommend new leads for you to contact based on connections between companies or people. It is possible for software algorithms to work out the relationship strength between different people, their interests, and whether they fit your ideal customer profile. In short, you can use AI for sales prospecting.

For example, there are tools that can help discover and recommend new leads to contact. These help eliminate the need for cold calls and give suggestions on who to contact, what to say to them, and when. They crawl the Internet, mining and mapping the connections between companies and people in the process. Not only do you get new potential leads, but they come with why they may have an interest in your products or services too.

By using prediction models, software tools can help learn and understand what prospects works best to target and reach out to them automatically from your email account. If you are interested in this, check out Node or Qualifier. Both companies offer solutions for sales prospecting. You may want to consider common tools available in more plain sight as well, such as LinkedIn's Sales Navigator tool and ability to propose new contacts based on your extended network. As we all know by now, the social media platforms are using AI-algorithms for most tasks these days.

You can also measure the relationship strength between your sales organization and a target account to determine the deal risk. You can get help identifying accounts where your relationships are weak or single-threaded. This is where you only have contact with one person at the company, which means they might be customers you are vulnerable to losing. One vendor providing relationship intelligence solutions is Nudge, which enables businesses to access new target accounts through their extended network and to analyze deal risk through precise relationship strength measurement.

I discussed their tool with Steve Woods, Co-Founder and CTO. He says that "Nudge gives an accurate assessment of pipeline health—where teams are 'single threaded' with just one strong relationship in an account. This enables sales to see where they lack access to the right roles in the buying center, which deals in forecast are most likely to slip."

Nudge performs analysis that can highlight gaps in relationship coverage. Those gaps can be resolved by giving sales teams full visibility into the relationships of the entire company, from executives all the way to service professionals. Woods elaborated further: "In order to do what we do, we need to create a map of all of the people and companies in the world. Then we can learn about how has relationships with whom. We use AI to piece together the signals of who everyone is and understand the result in terms of actual people working across different companies. Hence we can create a strong understanding of what relationships exist."

While AI tools for lead and customer acquisition may not replace your sales reps, they can surely improve work efficiency and reduce meaningless cold-calling to people who have no interest in what you offer. They can also help reduce risk of losing accounts with which you have a weak relationship. Other solutions mentioned elsewhere in this book can also help with lead generation or customer acquisition, either directly or indirectly. Read the sections on CRM data enrichment, conversion ratio optimization (CRO), chatbots, content marketing, and more for additional ideas.

Conversion Ratio Optimization

We don't want our marketing machinery to run idle. More specifically, we want our website to generate as many leads and customers as possible. This is where Conversion Ratio Optimization (CRO) comes in. It helps increase the number of people who take the next step towards a purchase. This can be any number of things.

For example, we may want to get as many people as possible to register with a form in return for a download of some sort, thus turning anonymous visitors into leads. This downloadable incentive used to get the contact information is commonly called a lead magnet. Similarly, we want as many leads as possible to turn into paying customers by clicking the purchase button on a sales page, or the checkout button in the web shop.

An important activity in CRO is testing different alternatives of important design objects. This may involve changing copy, imagery, button size, color or positioning, and more. The process of testing the best version of forms, landing pages, and sales pages is called A/B testing when two versions are tested against each other, and multivariate testing when many alternative versions compete with each other at the same time.

It is rumored that Google tried fifty-two different variations of blue for the hypertext links on their website, to test which color produced most clicks. Perhaps it is true, but it may be apocryphal. I suspect they test far more versions today, probably using genetic algorithms and machine learning. With machine learning, we can do automated A/B testing (or rather, massively large-scale multivariate testing) automatically. It becomes easy to test what combinations of colors, font, imagery, and positioning works best with your audience.

Using genetic algorithms, new design permutations to test can be generated automatically. Machine learning algorithms will determine which changes work best over time, and use that knowledge for further design permutations. Algorithms based on reinforcement learning can be useful here. As the tool proposes and tests new design variations using live website traffic, the algorithm is rewarded or punished for new design permutations dependent on if they improved the conversion ratio or not. In effect, reinforcement algorithms learn by trial and error. AI can thus be used to evolve winning website designs for automated CRO.

Some tools generate and test thousands of different design changes to work out which combination improves the conversion ratio the most. These tools may not only test how design changes on one page affects the conversion rate, but can also measure how a combination of design changes on several pages will produce best the result. Effectively, each visitor helps teach the system what works and what doesn't. This enables self-learning AI-driven designs that adapt to your audience and their changed behaviors automatically. This is what a product called Sentient Ascend does.

I had a conversation with Jeremy Miller, Vice President of Marketing at Sentient Technologies, to discuss AI-driven CRO. He gave an example of how this works. Their client, Cosabella, thought that 'free shipping' would perform better than 'family owned' at getting people to sign up to their newsletter. They were in fact wrong. It turned out their site visitors shared their same high regard for family values as they did. In just the first month and half of testing 160 designs, they already saw a 38% improvement in conversions. Such a large increase means a lot of money for some companies.

To do this, Ascend uses evolutionary computation that works similar to natural evolution. Different changes are introduced, and the ones producing better results survive. They are then used as the basis for a further generation of offspring that tries even better changes, and so on. Translated into Internet marketing and conversion ratio optimization, each web page is represented as a genome. Simulated genetic operators such as crossover and mutation are then performed. If the parent genomes are chosen among those that convert well, then some of their offspring genomes are likely to perform well too—perhaps even better than their parents. Each page permutation needs to be tested only to the extent that it is possible to decide whether it is promising (whether it should serve as a parent for the next generation) or should be discarded. I find this type of technology remarkable.

On the subject of automatic generation of webpage design, let's look at other options like Firedrop. This chatbot-based virtual web designer discusses the website project with you first in a chat window, and then auto-generates a complete website design based on your conversation. Other tools for AI-driven website design include The Grid, Wix Advanced Design Intelligence, and Bookmark.

Naser Alubaidi, Head of Marketing at Bookmark, explains his tool like this: "Bookmark uses genetic algorithms, machine learning and some human-assisted elements to provide every user with a website that is unique to them, their business and their industry. This is done by first getting some information about a user's business and then combining that with data gathered previously. The AI software will then make predictions on what sections, elements, images and pages this website should have based on the data gathered."

Bookmark's system gets smarter with every new website by learning from each user's choices and design decisions. Alubaidi says their mission is to make Bookmark the most experienced website designer in the world. They hope it will allow users to save at least 90% of their time and energy when creating and designing a website online. If they or someone else succeeds in doing this, then the market for web designers might plummet.

So far, we haven't seen many commercial solutions where AI is used to actually generate the creative, such as ad imagery or entire website designs. I think we will start to see more tools that generate this content automatically in the future, and Sentient and Bookmark are good examples of what is to come. Expect AI to assist in the design of ad creative as well in the near future.

Attribution Modeling

When talking about lead generation and customer acquisition, it may be of interest to consider the average customer acquisition cost (CAC) and customer lifetime value (CLTV). Knowing how much it will cost to acquire a new customer, and how much they are worth, are essential in being on top of your marketing strategy. It is also good to know how long time it takes for the average customer to pay back the acquisition cost.

In addition to monitoring your CAC and CLTV, you probably want to know what marketing activities contributed to the sale, as this helps measure the ROI of different marketing assets and initiatives. This is called attribution modeling and helps optimize the customer journey from a cost and results point of view.

The problem is, real life is seldom as easy as we might want. The customer journey is a multi-touch one, sometimes across many different channels and mediums. One particular ad, mailshot, or blog post may not be the sole reason someone bought a product. In fact, that would be highly unlikely. This is where attribution modeling comes in. It is an attempt to give credit to several marketing activities that all helped to acquire the customer. There are many different types of attribution models that give credit in different ways. For example:

- First touch attribution
- Lead conversion touch attribution
- Last touch attribution
- Last non-direct touch attribution

- Linear attribution
- Time decay attribution
- U-shaped attribution
- W-shaped attribution
- Full path attribution

One of the companies performing attribution modeling with machine learning is Cubed. I had a discussion with Russel McAthy, their CEO, to talk about his thoughts on this and to learn more about his company. He refers to his product as "a marketing analytics platform that helps businesses understand the performance of the full consumer journey—multi-visit and multi-device. It can be used as a single platform of truth, a place for all marketing channels and external data to be pulled into the same place to help inform the true story of how they impact revenue and value."

McAthy says his company's algorithm "means a shift from a last interaction/click world and into an attributed space. This allows smarter decision making with the ability to look at how activity truly impacts consumers as they are acquired, research and hopefully ultimately purchase."

Cubed uses a linear regression model, which we will discuss later, to look at the conversions. The algorithm goes through every single touch point that has happened prior to a successful conversion and is trained on the most impactful elements. A number of key factors on website pages are taken into consideration such as events that are triggered by the user as they engage marketing activities, including keywords, ads, and ultimately impression-led activities when users view creative on external websites.

Tools like this enable brands to invest in areas that truly add value to their consumers and drive incremental business growth. Other companies in this space are C3Metrics, ConversionLogic, VisualIQ, and Windsor (to my understanding, they aren't related to Windsor Circle, which also does AI-based marketing products). These companies also offer attribution modeling with machine learning for optimizing the cost efficiency of the customer journey.

Customer Relationships

Machine learning has many uses in customer relationship management, from email marketing, to social media engagement, to chatbots, and more. This section outlines a few ways artificial intelligence can be used to improve customer relationships.

Email Marketing

What is the first thing you do each morning? For me, it is reaching for my phone to check my emails. It is a terrible habit, I know, but I think most people are the same. This alone shows us that email is still relevant, and so is email marketing. It is one of the oldest forms of Internet marketing and is still going strong. As it turns out, prediction algorithms and machine learning are useful here too. With enough data, algorithms can measure what worked best in a campaign, and adapt and improve your email outreach over time.

One of the most common uses of AI in email, though separate from marketing, is a popular feature in Gmail. You might even have used it yourself! Gmail recommends suitable short replies to incoming email automatically with its smart reply technology. The Gmail inbox analyzes incoming messages with natural language processing (NLP) and natural language understanding (NLU) algorithms, and creates a suitable short response automatically using natural language generation (NLG). You can simply reply with the proposed text using a touch or click, or extend the reply by writing more in the auto-generated email draft.

A company called Conversica takes this concept further. They offer an AI-driven virtual assistant that initiates fully automated email correspondence with your leads in plain English. In effect, you get a virtual sales assistant that can send email messages back and forth, thereby nurturing your new leads into customers automatically. It is like a chatbot, but over email. With solutions like this, your sales reps can focus on the leads who are interested in buying, instead of wasting time of cold leads who will never covert. Your customer service team can also be relieved of answering common and simple questions.

I had a conversation with Gary Gerber, senior director and head of product marketing at Conversica. He says the platform combines natural language processing to understand incoming messages, an inference engine for basic decision-making, and natural language generation to create human-like messages. He says, "Think of all the money and resources being spent on marketing activities to drive that interest, and then not reaching people. So, an AI-based assistant, who will follow up with 100% of the leads as many times as it takes to engage them, makes perfect sense."

But does it work? His answer is to give an example from one of their customers: "Leveraging their AI assistant, the Los Angeles Film School generated a 33% increase in sales pipeline, which wouldn't have been humanly possible otherwise." Conversica works on mobile text (SMS) messages too.

A company called x.ai also does magic with email. They offer an AI-based scheduling assistant called Amy or Andrew, depending on your preference, that can be used for automated meeting bookings and scheduling of other things in the calendar. It does so by parsing your email correspondence automatically and integrating with your calendar. The main benefit here is to get rid of the endless email chains negotiating a phone or meeting time that works for both parties, or when rescheduling is needed. The scheduling robot can reach out to your contacts and propose a meeting, and it does the time selection negotiation for you using automated email correspondence and calendar integration.

We will probably see a lot of virtual sales and customer support assistants from an array of vendors in the near future, and it is interesting to see some of them are getting email and text/SMS capabilities as well, in addition to the more common chat windows. A crucial point is whether the natural language correspondence feels sufficiently human-like, of course. Your mileage may vary here, dependent on what solution you choose, but we can expect the bar will be raised significantly in this area in the coming years. It is only a matter of time before conversational AI-bots appear fully human, at least most of the time.

Let's move on to a completely different use of machine learning with emails. Marketing automation suppliers are beginning to use machine learning to optimize email send times individually for each recipient of an email broadcast. This helps improve email open rates and can help reduce the load on customer support centers as well. Seventh Sense goes even further to predict how frequently you should send to each contact in your database, optimizing email cadence based on their unique behavior and engagement patterns. In effect, this enables throttling of email delivery frequency to reduce email fatigue on a per-recipient basis.

Writing well-crafted email subject lines that give a high open rate has been an important task for improving email campaign results for years. Copywriters use their experience and gut feeling to come up with compelling subject lines that boost the likelihood recipients will open the email. Unopened emails will not help your marketing efforts, as we all know. In fact, writing compelling subject lines can be automated using AI, which optimize this step better than humans can. Examples of this are Phrasee and Persado, who offer language optimization solutions that uses machine learning to analyze historical response metrics and recommend subject lines that they think will have a higher open rate.

Self-optimizing subject lines are great, but it is possible to take this one step further. A potentially disruptive use of AI in email marketing is the automatic generation of email copy, hyper-personalized and optimized for engagement from each recipient. In fact, this personalization can go well beyond just the text. The imagery in the email can also be personalized based on the digital footprint of each recipient, or be dependent on external factors, like the current weather, football match results in the recipient's area, or other near real-time data that may be available.

A few years down the road, AI tools might even generate email graphics automatically using conversion optimization algorithms that know how to generate compelling images—hyper-personalized for each email recipient, of course. Boomtrain and OneSpot are examples of tool vendors that do email personalization. Their solutions include user behavior and content analysis to surface content that is likely to resonate well with a lead, and delivers it automatically using channels like email, the web, or push notifications.

Personalization is also available for product recommendations included in the email copy. An email can promote the product you are most likely to buy based on your previous behavior or other data. For example, I might be recommended red shorts in an email campaign from a clothing shop, whereas my neighbor gets an email that recommends blue t-shirts instead. Machine learning algorithms mine the digital footprint and other data to conclude which product each email recipient is most likely to buy next.

Many companies offer AI-based product recommendation systems, and I cover some of those in more detail in the section on product recommendations. You can also use machine learning to understand what email to send, to what person, at what time. This type of email sequence optimization is offered by companies like Optimail. This helps optimize the overall efficiency of automated drip email sequences.

Automatic generation of customer segments can also be done by machine learning algorithms to figure out what groups of contacts should receive a certain email campaign. I cover AI-based customer segmentation in another section of this book, but this directly applies to email marketing.

Not surprisingly, machine learning can be used for housekeeping duties too. A company called Siftrock uses machine learning to analyze email correspondence and update the lead and customer database automatically. For example, an AI bot can remove contacts that bounce (are no longer with a company), update contact information when someone has changed job title, mine phone numbers out of email footers, or scan out-of-office auto replies to find new leads within that company. This is done by integration with the existing CRM, emailing, or marketing automation system.

It is clear that machine learning has many uses for optimizing email content and improving email campaign performance overall, as well as leveraging email correspondence for completely different usages as well. Next, we'll look at how AI has and will continue to drive changes in social media, and how that can be used in your company.

Social Media

As social media has become increasingly important in our lives, so has social media marketing. This is why managers want to optimize their return on investment by monitoring how effective their social media strategies are. With a number of important social media platforms with users on them around the clock, it's impossible for a small company, even with dedicated social media specialists, to produce enough content to maintain a strong presence, or to monitor what is going on.

AI can help here. A number tools monitor social media activity and customer engagement for your company as well as your competitors. They then provide recommendations for how to optimize your social media outreach. Such machine learning tools can harvest massive amounts of data, process it automatically to uncover valuable patterns, and provide insights and recommended actions to improve your social media marketing results.

MeetCortex is one such vendor that aims to help you stop using ineffective social media content, and recommends what keywords, imagery, and hashtags inspire your audience the most. Cortex uses AI to build custom content calendars and content briefs for the coming months, then automatically populates it for human approval and scheduling. Furthermore, their tool can recommend how much to spend on paid promotions or boosting for each post to optimize your social media ad spending.

In a conversation I had with Brennan White, CEO and co-founder of MeetCortex, he shared some of his thoughts on using AI in marketing:

> *For marketing in particular, AI will have an immense impact and things marketers only dreamed about before will become possible (the individual-based, completely scalable marketing in Minority Report is possible with Cortex, for example). The ability to create bespoke content for each individual prospective customer and to target that content is now here. Ultimately, the experience of marketing for marketers will become much more effective and businesses will see a significant increase in marketing ROI.*

If you haven't seen Stephen Spielberg's *Minority Report* featuring Tom Cruise, now may be a good time. Note the personalized billboards and welcome displays in the store. Though this movie is only a few years old, science fiction is increasingly a reality these days, and AI is the key to this future.

Social media these days is primarily a visual medium, as most posts include imagery of some sort. The photos people publish often represent their interests and desires, demographics, and interests. This is a treasure trove to mine for marketing insights! An innovative company in the image recognition space is Netra. Their system detects customer preferences, interests, and demographics from photos on social media, thus helping companies understand their audience and how to reach them in a better way. In effect, they add visual intelligence and insights that go beyond text-based analytics.

Another vendor offering AI-powered social analytics with image analysis is Crimson Hexagon, whose cloud service helps companies uncover insights from social media data. This is to understand audiences, track brand perception, and detect competitive and market trends to help drive strategy decisions. Their tool uses over 1 trillion social media posts, machine learning, and image and sentiment analysis to get deep audience insights. This helps understand the audience, identify growth strategies, and improve campaign results.

Data inputs for the consumer conversations monitored include public online social media (Twitter, Reddit, Facebook, etc.), enterprise-held data (ratings and reviews, support tickets, call transcripts), and other public online data (Bloomberg, Yahoo Finance).

Jane Zupan, Senior Director of Product Marketing at Crimson Hexagon, says her company "helps clients by continually monitoring public online conversations and sending alerts if there is an anomaly in the typical pattern, such as a sudden shift in the volume of conversation around the brand, or a change in the general sentiment, such as a spike in anger or joy. The user can drill down deeper to determine the cause of the anomaly or the shift, and better understand the perceptions and motivations for their audience." Certainly, marketing departments have no shortage of powerful large-scale analytics tools today.

AI-based systems can also help protect your brand online by monitoring millions of user generated comments for negative sentiment, as well as removing spam, unwanted ads, links, personal information, profanity, and other problematic content from your profiles across the Internet. A company called Smart Moderation does this by offering an AI-powered system for comment moderation, shielding social media accounts, forums, and blog comments from abusive language and Internet trolls.

Ciler Ay, CEO of Smart Moderation, says that "Communities shouldn't feel compelled to silence or censor themselves to avoid abuse. We see it as imperative to help individuals enforce community guidelines in order to foster open, respectful discussion." This is a noble goal, and tools helping with this are getting increasingly important as trolls and online bullying become more common.

To implement this functionality, Smart Moderation uses an AI architecture based on machine learning and natural language processing that reads the meaning and tone behind a message rather than relying on static keyword blacklists. The technology becomes self-learning and adapts and customizes itself to users' past actions and preferences, profile by profile.

Another company, Movyl Technologies, offers an AI-based social marketing platform that analyses campaigns and automates many of the labor-intensive tasks involved in outreach, like composing, scheduling, and publishing content. Using machine learning, the platform learns how to undertake many of these tasks itself without extensive human guidance and offers insights to help marketing teams broaden reach and engagement with customers.

Finally, the elephant in the room here is of course the social media platforms themselves. Virtually all social media platforms, like Facebook or LinkedIn, uses artificial intelligence in their algorithms. The word algorithm can make any social media manager look terrified these days. In short, social media channels are using machine learning algorithms to limit the visibility of your organic posts in an attempt to throttle the vast amounts of post that scroll by in the feeds. We'll learn more about algorithms later, but for now, the products we've covered here can help your company make the most of your social media outreach.

Chatbots

Chatbots are one of the hottest areas in Internet marketing right now. These are software components that know how to keep a seemingly intelligent conversation with your leads and customers, for example by offering 24/7 autonomous customer service. Machine leaning, natural language processing (NLP), natural language understanding (NLU), and natural language generation (NLG) are used to understand and drive the correspondence forward, sometimes in combination with sentiment analysis to understand the emotional mood of the user.

A chatbot is usually found in a chat window on your website, in social media platforms like Facebook or Twitter, or in messaging platforms like Apple iMessage or Slack. Chatbots are often used for customer service and can help by answering basic questions automatically. Depending on the industry, a chatbot may be able to answer 50-80% of incoming customer service enquiries automatically. What's more, they are on duty around the clock and never need a coffee break.

The chatbot can either be statically programmed to know predetermined answers to common questions, like "when does the restaurant close on Thursdays?" or "do you have free parking?", or have dynamic database lookup capabilities, for example checking and responding with the price of a car insurance for a vehicle with a specific license plate number, or the price of a hotel room on a particular date. Some chatbots can hand over the correspondence to a human agent, should it detect it is unable to cope with the situation. This may be the best of both worlds, thus providing automation of simple customer service queries at scale, combined with human care in case of difficult matters.

Chatbots don't just have to be customer service agents, though. Growthbot is an interesting example. This marketing and sales agent integrates into Slack, Facebook Messenger, and Twitter. It was created by Dharmesh Shah, the legendary co-founder and CTO of HubSpot, and it can give you quick, easy access to information and services related to growing a business, sales, marketing, and more.

Another great example is eBay's chatbot (or shopbot, as they call it) inside Facebook Messenger. They position it as a virtual personal shopper, and you can have natural conversation with it in plain English. You can say things like "show me red jogging shoes under $100" and it will ask about shoe size and whether it is for a man or woman, and other relevant questions. Once the shopbot has filtered down the query sufficiently, it presents a number of product recommendations, each with a photo, product description, price, and perhaps other information.

If you like one of them, only a touch is required to add it to the shopping cart and purchase it. If you don't, you can say things like "show more models," "similar but in blue," "the same but in size 42" and more—all within the familiar environment of Facebook Messenger. It also remembers your shopping habits, like shoe size and gender, and improves its product recommendations over time based on your preferences. This gives it an edge on simply searching an online store using keywords by automating the interaction and learning over time how to better help you.

One of the coolest features of eBay's shopping bot is the ability to upload a photo containing something you would like to buy. Say you pass a shop and see something you like, or want to get the same T-shirt as a friend. Using the eBay shopbot, you can take a photo of the desired object, upload it, and the shopbot will detect it using image recognition technology. It then presents products that look the same and can be bought on eBay. Similarly, Google now has Lens, which can analyze a picture taken with your phone camera and present information on the item, like the price and where to purchase it.

This technology is incredible, and many predict chatbots or shopbots integrated into Facebook Messenger, Apple iMessage, and other platforms will replace traditional web shops as the preferred mechanism for online shopping and e-commerce in the next few years. This paradigm shift may be boosted by the emergence of natural voice control with full conversational capabilities. If you want to make purchases online using voice, you will need a chatbot to do so.

In fact, voice-based assistants like Apple Siri, Amazon Alexa, Microsoft Cortana, and Google Assistant are becoming increasingly popular, propelled in part by smart speakers like Apple HomePod, Amazon Echo, and Google Home. These are continuously listening to your requests in your home. It isn't hard to imagine the equivalent of an eBay shopbot integrated into these voice assistants. I predict these voice-based assistants will be integrated into many other products outside of smart speakers in the future, like refrigerators, TVs, cars, and more. You can then simply buy new detergent—or virtually any other product—using a short voice conversation.

With Google Duplex, this is taken one step further. Or rather, the issue is reversed. Instead of having a voice-based chatbot listening to requests for services, Google Duplex is a voice assistant that can initiate phone calls and have automated, natural voice conversations with people on the other end. When presenting Duplex at Google I/O in May 2018, a demo showed how the software made phone calls to hair salons and restaurants, negotiating an appointment for a haircut and a restaurant reservation, respectively.

With voice-based chatbots initiating outbound phone calls, there may soon be no need for call centers. A voice-based chatbot can easily dial and manage thousands of phone conversations in parallel, removing vast numbers of call center jobs in the process. It also allows for improved service and cost reductions if the chatbot speaks many languages, thus removing the need for translators or multi-lingual staff. The possibilities are endless. For example, automatic calls informing customers about changed delivery schedules or flight delays, calling parents informing that the teacher is sick and the kids have to stay at home from school, or unmanned phone surveys—all with the nuance and personalization of a real human.

In fact, voice interfaces may disrupt the online industry by making traditional web pages far less important. If people interact with internet services verbally, they will be less likely to turn to traditional websites to search for information. If you're sitting on your couch and want to find the closest pizza restaurant, it's far easier to speak the command to your voice-activated home assistant device than to bring up a search on your phone or laptop. That would disrupt the search engine optimization (SEO) industry, to start with. If voice assistants rather than web pages become the main interface to the internet in the future, then ad-financed companies like Google and Facebook may be in for a massive reduction in revenue. As an example, how would Google monetize search ads (Google Adwords) from a voice interface? I don't think the users would accept ten ads being read aloud before the answer to a search is presented.

The future truly is here. In fact, you can already add speech recognition to your own products. Amazon pioneered the option to inject your own services into Amazon Alexa. Using a feature called Skills, any company can add voice commands to Amazon's system. The Google counterparts are called Actions.

An interesting example of this is the Swedish company LogTrade, which develops cloud-based software for digital logistics (ordering and management of freight services). LogTrade developed their own Alexa Skills and Google Actions, meaning that their customers can now order shipments or query for freight status using simple voice commands. This provides unprecedented convenience in many situations, particularly if you can't use your hands to type on a keyboard for whatever reason. You might be driving a fork lift, for example, or wearing protective gear.

In June 2017, Apple announced a similar "hook-in" capability for its iMessage text service called "Business chat" or "Chatbots for iMessage". Chatbots built using this technology can integrate with the rest of iOS, and schedule meetings in the calendar or initiate payments using Apple Pay. Using this tool, airlines could allow ticket purchase and seat selection, and hotels could allow you to book rooms, all from within Apple iMessage.

How do you develop a chatbot or shopbot for your business and have it integrated into popular platforms like Facebook Messenger, Twitter, Slack, Alexa, or Siri? The companies offering chatbot integration with their products have opened up this capability using APIs (application programming interfaces), enabling software developers to hook in their own functionality. The easiest solution is to use a chatbot development platform, which is effectively a high-level chatbot authoring tool that can be used to develop these systems with a minimum of programming expertise.

It took me just a few hours to develop my first chatbot. I used Motion.AI (now acquired by HubSpot) and designed the conversational flow by building a state-chart using graphical drag and drop tools. Most other chatbot development tools are similarly easy to use. They then transparently integrate with the chat platforms (Facebook Messenger, Apple iMessage, Slack, etc.), completely removing the need for you to understand how to do this manually.

Many of these chatbot authoring tools offer a "design-once, deploy on many platforms" approach, further increasing their appeal. This means your chatbot only has to be developed one time, but can be deployed more or less automatically in many different chat platforms. Examples of such solutions include Chatfuel, Flow XO, ChattyPeople, ManyChat, Octane.ai, and many more. IBM Watson, Microsoft Bot Framework, and Microsoft Language Understanding Intelligent Service (LUIS) are other solutions from major players in the industry.

In fact, there are now so many options available in this space, that I can't list them all. A Google search on "chatbot development tools" should give you a place to start. One of the reasons there are so many available is the importance many think chatbots will have in the years to come. You may want to monitor this, or perhaps get your own chatbot developed right away. I have to say it was immensely rewarding to talk with a virtual copy of myself the first time I developed my own chatbot.

Now, let's move on to discuss how AI can help marketers in other ways.

Customer Service

AI and machine learning can be used to augment or replace humans in customer service to reduce average handling time and improve service quality. Most people think about conversational chatbots for this, but AI-based natural language processing can be used to improve or automate customer service in other ways.

Two examples are Kylie and TrueAI, which both analyse past customer service interactions and learn how to respond to questions that have occured in the past. They propose suitable answers automatically and offer them as a help to service agents. This may be particularly helpful while training new service agents. Since these are not unattended bot solutions, the service agent is still in control and receives AI assistance in crafting suitable answers and improving their efficiency with routine tasks.

Scanning incoming email can be a time-consuming task in many companies. Some vendors, for example Digital Genius, offer solutions that can parse incoming email and route them to the correct department automatically, dependent on the detected topic. This additional layer of automation reduces workload and improves efficiency.

For customer service over phone, companies like Cogito and TalkIq can analyze and augment ongoing phone calls, thus working to improve conversations with behavioral science. The customer's voice can be analyzed for attributes like energy, interruption, empathy, participation, pace, and more. This data is used to help gain further insights, for example guiding agents to speak with more empathy or confidence, as early signs of customer frustration is detected.

A company called Chorus uses a system that records and analyses voices too, but they focus on creating summaries of each sales-meeting (physical, phone calls, or in the form of webinars) in real-time, automatically identifying important topics being discussed and providing meeting performance metrics. Effectively, they take a data-driven and AI-based approach to improving meeting efficiency.

Contact Enrichment

Most companies use Customer Relationship Management (CRM) systems these days, at least in the B2B space. These systems can be made more efficient if the customer data are enriched with supplementary data from external sources to provide sales reps with better insights on leads and prospects. This is why CRM tool suppliers like Salesforce and HubSpot are moving into AI to make contact management more efficient. This is no surprise, of course, and we've seen Salesforce pushing their Einstein system, while HubSpot acquired Kemvi. Clearly, there are strong financial incentives for them to do so.

In a whitepaper from June 2017, "A Trillion-Dollar Boost: The Economic Impact of AI on Customer Relationship Management," IDC calculates that "AI associated with CRM activities will boost global business revenue from the beginning of 2017 to the end of 2021 by $1.1 trillion … Net-new jobs associated with this revenue could, if respondent opinions bear out, reach more than 800,000 by 2021 in direct jobs, and 2 million if you add in indirect and induced jobs. This is a net-positive figure in that it includes an estimate of jobs lost to automation from AI."[11]

This is big money, any way you see it. How can AI help do this? Large manually managed customer relationship databases are like searching for a needle in the haystack; it is very time consuming to find the prospects most likely to convert and to annotate all activities with a lead. With AI-infused insights and contact data enrichment, you are much more likely to focus on the leads that are close to making a purchase. You can generate and monitor more information and insights about them while spending less time in the process.

AI can be used to enrich the customer data you have in your CRM system, thus filling data voids. Tools performing such tricks can arm a sales team with customer information collected from a large number of

---

11 "A Trillion-Dollar Boost: The Economic Impact of AI on Customer Relationship Management," IDC, June 2017. *https://www.salesforce.com/content/dam/web/en_us/www/documents/white-papers/the-economic-impact-of-ai.pdf*

external sources, dramatically improving the effectiveness of finding and understanding the background and activities of each lead.

With AI-assisted CRM, tools can harvest data and highlight useful information like identifying new leads or source contact information and predict what content or activities might have the best results with each person. This helps you to prioritize which leads to spend time with. Many companies can harvest data from hundreds of data sources, cleaning, unifying and enriching customer data in real-time. Examples include Zylotech, Squirro, Maroon, Smarter Codes, and Everstring.

AI can also be used to analyze and improve the sales organization itself. People.ai provides tools for this. They promote a solution that detects what activities and behaviors lead to repeatable sales success and provides a rep-based and account-based view of the sales process. This solution can be used by sales managers to coach sales reps for improved future sales results.

In the last few sections, we've looked at a number of examples of how AI can be used to improve customer relationships. Now, let's see how artificial intelligence can help us understand the customers better.

Knowing Your Customer

Good marketers always listen to their customers. This can be done in many shapes and forms. The traditional way is to talk to them in person or over phone and collect direct or indirect feedback. It can also be done using surveys and questionnaires. In the digital age, there are many more ways to listen to the voice of the customer, and with artificial intelligence, we can do things we never thought possible a decade ago.

Why is it important to listen to the customer? Because by the time they leave, it is too late to rectify the situation. Customer churn is the final cry. Unhappy customers often show signs that they are unhappy long before they leave you. How can you detect this? There are many ways, including measuring:

- The number of website and blog returns and visitor behavior
- The number of web shop visits and shopping behavior
- Email opens and clicks
- Open rates for push notifications

- Social media engagement
- Customer service interactions
- Recommendations and reviews
- Sentiment analysis of interactions
- Conversion rates
- The emotional state of your customers

While many such measurements are not based on AI per se, the accuracy of your reporting can be improved by using predictive marketing and machine learning, thus providing new ways to hear the customer's voice. You can then measure the difference in behavior for highly personalized content versus static mass-audience content. The personalized outreach is likely more efficient and can lead to deeper relationships with your customers.

Customer Sentiment

With modern tools, you can get insights never before imaginable. Sentiment analysis is one of those areas. This is about detecting emotions in text to better understand how customers feel about your products, and their opinions and needs. With sentiment analysis (also known as emotional AI, or opinion mining), you can measure if someone is positive, negative, or neutral towards your brand or product, and what emotional state they may be in.

In effect, you get to know how they feel when they write about your brand or products. This information is gathered by analyzing and understanding text in email, social media posts, product reviews, customer service tickets, chatbot conversations, and more using natural language processing and natural language understanding. In short, you can see the polarity of their opinions, and how strong those opinions are.

A company in the text analytics space is Lexalytics. They have offered commercial sentiment analytics software since 2004 and their system processes billions of documents per day. Their solution analyzes and provides insights around a company's text data from surveys, call logs, social media posts, message boards, and comments. In addition to the more common cloud-based or on-premises solutions for text and sentiment analysis, they also offer an add-in for Microsoft Excel to easily analyze both structured and unstructured survey data, generate insights, and create reports and data visualizations.

I spoke with Seth Redmore, CMO of Lexalytics. He argues there's simply too much human communication out there to understand, analyze, and act on without AI assistance. To address this, he says, "The Lexalytics Intelligence Platform helps businesses work better with text. This could be as part of a decision support system, or an analytics offering, or predictions. It could be looking backwards, or peering forwards."

Redmore explained that "Text is language. To understand text is to understand meaning, in a way, it is to understand the nature of being human, by being able to untangle how we communicate. We focus on conversational text—as examples, social media or customer feedback."

We will see businesses harvesting more insights from text and sentiment analysis in the years to come. There are many vendors in the field, all with different strengths and weaknesses. In general, they all use natural language processing algorithms to enable their magic. Depending what solution you chose, your experience may differ in terms of languages supported, or how advanced the language understanding is. Some products might only support English, which may be a problem to companies in non-English speaking countries.

Talkwalker, a social media analytics company, launched an AI-based sentiment analysis tool in the autumn of 2017 that claims to detect customer sentiment with 90% accuracy, even understanding irony and sarcasm. With machine learning, the tool understands the meaning of full sentences and determines the attitude in social media posts or other content. Their platform monitors and analyzes online conversations in real time across social networks, news websites, blogs, and forums—all in 187 languages.

The analytics engine analyzes the data across a wide variety of categories including social engagement level, sentiment, demographics, location, linked themes, and more. It also features image analytics technology and sentiment analysis. Christophe Folshette, co-founder of Talkwalker, explains that, "All of Talkwalker's AI technology is proprietary and is currently focused on image analytics capabilities, sentiment analysis and data classification. Talkwalker's image analysis is able to detect not only brand logos, but also scenes and objects within images to give clients greater clarity on the context these images are used in."

Folshette goes on to say, "We've rapidly increased our AI-based image applications, adding scenery, objects, gender and age detection. We're seeing clients use this technology for a wide range of purposes from understanding the impact of sponsorship to analyzing Instagram data to create maps of customer tastes and preferences and direct business expansion."

Companies with the right AI-powered tools certainly seem to have better insights to base their decisions upon, but that's not the end of the possibilities. Sentiment analysis can be applied to audio as well. One example is the phone service company Nexmo, which provides real-time customer sentiment analysis of voice calls. A voice-based AI-bot monitors the conversation and estimates the emotions of calling customers. The service agent can watch the estimated customer sentiment live as the call progresses, then react to change the course of the call as needed.

Another machine learning solution that goes beyond words is Affectiva. They can analyze the emotional state of facial expressions in images, while Beyond Verbal does something similar thing voice recordings. These types of tools can help analyze how people feel based on images or audio recordings. Given the vast amounts of footprints leads and customers leave in text, audio, and images, there is no shortage of data to harvest for emotional intelligence. As these systems develop and become ubiquitous, we as a society will need to think and act clearly on the legal and ethical aspects of these systems.

Churn Prediction and Customer Retention

Most businesses suffer from churn—that is, customers who defect and stop purchasing your products or services. This is a major problem, as conventional wisdom commonly claims it is about five or six times as expensive to recruit a new customer compared to keeping an existing one. Existing customers are also more likely to buy additional products from you. Understanding why customers stop purchasing and assessing the risks are key aspects of a data-driven retention strategy.

Churn prediction may be particularly important to companies offering subscription plans, such as mobile phone operators or cloud software vendors. To them, it is of utmost importance to keep the subscription plans active as long as possible. Detecting unhappy customers early gives you the opportunity to offer incentives to stay. In effect, if you know in advance which customers are likely going to abandon you, you can reach out to them ahead of time and try to prevent this from happening.

With AI-driven predictive marketing, it is often possible to detect what factors and patterns indicate a customer is likely to leave. Dependent on the customer value, AI-driven churn prediction algorithms could trigger the marketing automation system to send a sequence of nurturing emails, possibly with a discount offer to re-engage the customer. This might be a suitable approach for low-value customers and in the B2C market, but for your best customers in a B2B market, the predictive marketing system might instead be configured to notify a sales representative to make a personal call to the customer and try to rectify the situation before it happens.

Churn can be detected by analyzing factors like:

- Demographic data
- Digital footprint (website/email behavior, etc.)
- Purchase history and payment patterns
- Social media sentiment analysis
- Product usage patterns, if measurable
- Customer support statistics

To detect churn, we simply want to know how likely each customer is to defect. Classification algorithms like decision trees can be used for this, as they can classify a customer into one of two categories, based on their behavior and that of other customers. In our case, we interpret the two classes as "likely to defect" and "not likely to defect". We can then act upon these insights accordingly to keep the customer longer. Many commercial vendors offer churn prediction tools, for example Optimove, Peak, and DeepSense. Omni-channel customer data platforms (CDPs) benefit from this functionality as well.

Part of predicting customer churn is to learn how to act upon such insights. Customer retention is the mix of activities you can take to reduce churn and retain as many customers as you can through customer care, purchase incentives, loyalty programs, or other means. Retention is an ongoing process throughout the lifetime of the customer relationship and should not be bolted on at the end as a solution to an otherwise failing customer experience. Having said that, retention and loyalty programs may help keep your customers, or reactivate them once they have defected.

Predictive Lead Scoring

Having too many leads may appear to be a good thing. In fact, most CMOs would love to have this problem. However, being flooded by leads unlikely to buy is a problem in itself, as they bog down your sales time, thus damaging sales activities towards potential customers more likely to buy. There is a significant difference in being flooded by poor leads versus having quality leads who are just a bit too early in the funnel.

There are two solutions to the first situation: either you get rid of the low-quality leads altogether, or you filter them out. In the second situation, you have quality leads worth nurturing, but they aren't yet ready to purchase. With a stretched sales organization, both situations lead to the same conclusion: your valuable sales reps ought to focus on the right leads. In practice, this means prioritizing the leads most likely to purchase soon. The other leads might be nurtured using traditional marketing automation systems until they become warmer.

How do you do this filtering and prioritization? Traditionally, marketing automation systems allowed manually configured lead scoring algorithms to rate the leads versus each other. This is done by attaching credits to various activities. Recurring website visits and certain page views increased the lead score. For example, it might be +1 for each page view, but visiting the pricing page gives +10, and a visit to the job opportunities page gives -15 (since the user's interest isn't in the product). Every PDF download may give +10, and watching a video on the website gives +5, and so on.

You get the point. Various activities add or subtract to the lead score, and the total lead score gives a rating of how "hot" a particular lead is estimated to be. This is great in theory, but is subject to certain problems. For example, the manually designed scoring formula might give the wrong perception of how likely a lead is to purchase. You may assume that certain types of page views are more or less important than they really are. You may think that downloading PDF documents is a stronger purchase signal than something else. Sometimes, these assumptions are wrong.

This is where machine learning and predictive lead scoring comes to the rescue. With predictive lead scoring, a software algorithm compares the past behavior of those who later became customers with a particular new lead who is not yet a customer. In effect, the digital behaviors of a lead are compared to the behaviors of actual customers before they became customers. Depending on the similarity in behavior, a lead score (usually in the range 0-100%) is calculated to assess how likely a new lead is to become a paying customer.

For leads passing the threshold of a lead score about 25%, a marketing automation system may send a sequence of nurturing emails with a soft sales message. Leads having a lead score over 50% may get emails with a harder sales message. Those with a lead score about 75% may be put in the queue for manual follow-up by a sales rep. Several software tools perform predictive lead scoring like this. Many marketing automation systems and CRM systems, including HubSpot, Marketo, and SalesForce can do this too.

Infer (now acquired by Ignite Technologies) is one of the vendors who offer dedicated predictive lead scoring solutions, thus helping the sales team focus on opportunities with the highest probability of closing. They use a combination of data gathering and machine learning to classify and rank leads and accounts on the likelihood that they will convert. I asked Rob Franks, Vice President of Professional Services at Ignite Technologies, how this happens.

He says, "Infer works by gathering data, called signals, about the lead from over 4000 different sources. The sources include syndicated data providers, proprietary data gathered from web crawling and the inputs and behaviors of the customer. Initial models are built by taking a history of data, classifying the signals and using win loss history to train a predictive model."

In essence, the prediction algorithm learns what lead behaviors and attributes have led to a won or lost deal in the past, and uses that to assess new leads. Franks explains, "The models are reviewed and optimized in Infer's proprietary workbench tool by experienced data analysts and scientists. When the model is ready, it is deployed to score all active leads and new leads as they are created. Scores can change as signals evolve so the models are periodically re-built with a more recent history of wins."

I've used predictive lead scoring myself for a few years, and it is indeed a handy solution to filter out what are predicted to be low-quality leads. It is also great to use different lead scoring thresholds in marketing automation workflow trigger conditions. As mentioned above, a marketing automation system may send different types of messages to clients with different leads scores.

Many other vendors offer predictive lead scoring systems, including Lattice, Maroon, and Mintigo, and several CRM system suppliers we discussed above. You will have to assess what system works best for your organization. In my experience, predictive leads scoring works well in combination with marketing automation workflows. You can use lead scoring alone to prioritize leads for manual outreach or as a handover threshold from marketing to sales, but automated email sequences or other workflow logic makes this capability shine.

Mass-Marketing and the Segment of One

With machine learning, it becomes feasible to personalize content and outreach strategies to each individual contact, which helps make marketing more relevant. In fact, personalization is one of the most important uses for artificial intelligence in marketing. Over the next five sections, we'll look at some of the most common ways AI can be used in this context.

Segmentation

The time of spammy "spray and pray" mass-marketing is over. Today's customers require brands—and expect marketing outreach—to be more relevant in both time and content. Relevancy is becoming more important than reach; get the right content, to the right person, at the right time. Marketers tried to become more relevant by inventing the concept of segmentation. Groups of customers or potential customers are placed into distinct sub-groups, thus making a rough classification by similarity or common needs. Segmentation made it possible for marketers to be at least a bit more relevant, compared to sending the same marketing emails or offers to everyone.

I know a clothing retail chain that did this rather poorly, sending marketing emails pitching women's clothes to men and vice versa. They sent exactly the same email to everyone. Another retail chain sent direct marketing information on gardening products to people living in an apartment, thus not having a garden. These are significant blunders in today's era, and brands just have to do better. When you send irrelevant marketing content to your leads, you train them to avoid reading it in the future, or even make them dislike you. That in turn can harm your email sender score, thus damaging the delivery rate of future emails. Even the most trivial segmentation—like sending different product offers to men or women—can make a major difference. Still, men are not a homogenous group, and they have different needs and interests, as do women. A more granular segmentation would thus result in even more relevance.

With AI and machine learning, it is possible to segment the audience automatically. If this is done with sufficient granularity, we get micro-segmentation. Done correctly, this is much better than no segmentation, or rudimentary segmentation. AI-based automatic segmentation can be implemented using clustering algorithms, and can identify the attributes of ideal buyers, those most likely to convert or defect, and more. In effect, you can ask the system to provide you with buckets of people that are similar or share characteristics in some way, even if you don't know what you are looking for. Thus, machine learning tools can help improve segmentation, and many do. However, other tools focus on another approach called the "segment of one."

Predictive Content and Personalization

Segmentation taken to the extreme eventually creates segments of one. This personalization allows for dramatically more effective campaigns. It allows you to send content and offers that are uniquely optimized for every individual person. This is called the segment of one (or audience of one), denoting a hyper-personalized outreach where the message is uniquely modified and optimized for each person. This would certainly make marketing more relevant!

In fact, personalization is the opposite of segmentation. With segmentation, we create groups of people with similar attributes and send the same messages to all of them. By definition, this is not personalized for each individual, even with micro-segmentation. With personalization, we want each message to be truly unique. It is actually adjusted and optimized for each individual using prediction algorithms. There are already many vendors offering AI-based personalization systems. The majority of these tools can personalize the content on web pages or email content.

They do this by using machine learning algorithms to predict what customers want and deliver relevant content or product recommendations even before they ask. The "Personalization in Shopping" report notes that "Shopper spend soars with personalization. Purchases where a recommendation was clicked saw a 10% higher average order value, and the per-visit spend of a shopper who clicks a recommendation is five times higher."[12]

The report further states, "Providing your customers with a personalized shopping experience is now the cost of entry to retail." It reports that 50% of customers say they are likely to switch vendor if a company doesn't foresee their needs, and 58% of consumers say technology has considerably altered their expectations of what customer experience companies shall give them. Personalization is now a requirement for any company wanting to stay with the times. I think we can conclude that it isn't optional anymore, but rather a pre-requisite to matching your competitors.

However, it isn't just about recommending content, products or offers. It is about creating customer experiences that build engagement and drive retention. It's about appearing less robotic and being more personal and relevant. Personalization will be huge in the marketing industry. In

---

12   "Personalization in Shopping," Salesforce, 2017. *https://www.demandware.com/uploads/resources/REP__Personalization_in_Shopping_EN_31OCT2017_FINAL_EK_.pdf*

fact, the future of marketing technology and the vendor landscape might well be an arms race for better personalization.

Many companies have developed AI-based technology that uses user behavior and content analysis to deliver the content that is most likely to resonate with a particular person. Most of them offer solutions for the personalization of web page and email content. Some go beyond that to support additional communication channels. A few prominent companies in this space include Zeta (previously BoomTrain), Adobe Marketing Cloud, Emarsys, and Perzonalization.

I asked Lindsay Tjepkema, Global Head of Content for Emarsys, to explain their product. She noted that "Emarsys is a marketing cloud which provides AI based personalization across email, SMS, mobile, web, offline and IoT devices." The platform consolidates all web, mobile, email, and purchase information into a unified customer profile. This profile includes preferences, behavior trends, predicted behaviors, propensities, and affinities. The unified profile is the platform's foundation—the "single source of truth"—which enables hyper-personalization across all channels. Tjepkema continues: "As the real-time interactions scale, the need for content increases exponentially. Marketers will have to offload the technology tasks such as identifying segments, crafting journeys, and creating campaigns. They will have to concentrate purely on creating content and training machines on marketing strategies."

Other companies avoid developing their own proprietary AI by building their products on the back of existing engines. OpenTopic takes this route, as their tool is built on top of IBM's AI engine, Watson. The computing power of Watson is used to predict the most engaging assets that guide individuals through the customer journey.

In addition to the more traditional content recommendation functionalities, Dynamic Yield, Klevu, PureClarity, and Similar add personalization to search results as well. Dependent on what you have done before, you will get different search results on an e-commerce site, compared to your neighbor searching for the same thing.

I spoke with Mike Mallazzo, the head of content at Dynamic Yield. He points out that in its annual "What's Hot in Digital Commerce" report, Gartner cited personalization as the number one strategic investment for brands in 2017. McKinsey, he said, refers to digital personalization at scale as "marketing's holy grail," and the Boston Consulting Group predicts that personalization will push an $800 billion revenue shift to the 15% of brands that get it right in the next five years. The message from the marketplace is clear: personalization is no longer just nice to have; it is the single most important strategy for boosting revenue and brand affinity online. Expect predictive content and hyper-personalization to be a major deal going forward.

Malazzo also discussed what helps set his company's product apart: "Marketers can turn control over to the machines or insert guardrails in the form of merchandising rules to control which recommendations unit each visitor sees. For example, a high-end fashion brand may want our AI to recommend the products delivering the most revenue but may not want to place certain brands next to each other. In Dynamic Yield, it is possible to set this condition, allowing the machines to go to work within controls set by the marketer."

The companion to personalization is recommendation. Whereas the former selects individualized ads or content, the latter uses data and machine learning to anticipate what products may interest you while shopping. While personalization and recommendation engines arguably are two sides of the same coin, the distinction helps us to understand these systems. Let's study the latter a bit more.

Recommendation Engines

While content marketers are interested in adaptive and predictive content, e-commerce marketers might be more interested in the product recommendations that optimize sales and maximize revenue. Amazon is the master of this, and their team uses machine learning to personalize product recommendations based on digital footprint and previous purchase history—both from you and others. Features like "You may also like this" and "Other people also bought" that were popularized by Amazon are becoming the norm in e-commerce these days.

The "Personalization in Shopping" report also notes, "Recommendations are directly linked to longer shopping visits. Shoppers that clicked a product recommendation spent an average of 12.9 minutes on-site vs. 2.9 minutes for those that didn't click recommendations." Of course, when they stay longer on the site, they spend more too.

The report states that "visits where the shopper clicked a recommendation comprise just 7% of all visits, but 24% of orders and 26% of revenue." Shoppers that click recommendations view 4.8 times more products and spend five times more per visit. Furthermore, 52% of orders from recommendation-clickers include one of the recommended items. These figures seem to be a good argument for the use of recommendation engines in e-commerce.

Luckily, nearly all e-commerce site, even small ones, can now use AI-driven product recommendations that are optimized and adapted for each individual person. The suggestions can come in many forms, but generally, they adapt the products each specific person is offered on websites or in email.

There are many popular e-commerce platforms in widespread use including Shopify, OpenCart, WooCommerce, PrestaShop, and Magento. Wouldn't it be nice to get a product recommendation engine for the system that drives your business? You can use companies like BlueShift, Dynamic Yield, Perzonalization, Reflektion, RetentionScience, and Zen to help increase sales by personalized product recommendations, including the display of similar products, trending (most popular) products, top picks for you, recently viewed, often bought together, and the like. Up-selling and cross-selling is also a common feature here.

Do you want to extend recommendations beyond products and e-commerce? The same type of predictive technology can be used to recommend what content (such as CTAs, banner ads, lead magnets, and other downloadable resources) to display on your website for a particular visitor. Certona, Marketo, and Uberflip do this effectively, helping to promote your content library in a smarter way.

Recommendation engines have many more uses. For example, they can be integrated into the products themselves. Netflix is a great example, and their recommendations for movies you might want to watch are a contributing factor for their huge success. You might be able to replicate some of that magic by using recommendation engines appropriately in your business.

Audience Management

With audience AI and hyper-dynamic targeting, machine learning can be used to help build targeted audiences automatically. This is done by using data from a variety of sources and making predictions about the characteristics of ideal buyers. In a few seconds, you can get well-targeted, quality audiences, with a high likelihood of more conversions and sales. Audience AI learns how to find the best customers across various channels, such as social media. As more data becomes available, the targeting becomes increasingly precise.

These tools can uncover the motivations and desires of target audiences, sometimes finding passion points with interest analysis, core values, and personality traits with personality analysis, and using visual imagery analysis to work out what pictures or creative elements engage the target audience the most. Some products performing these types of tricks are the well-known behemoths like Salesforce and Adobe, but also specialized companies like Codec, Leadspace, Toneden, and Trapica. Of course, we can't forget the ads platform on Facebook and other social media sites. AI can be useful in audience management, particularly for companies with large customer volumes, as often is the case in the B2C space.

The Customer Journey

Many of the AI solutions available to marketers focus on a specific problem, such as email send times or conversion ratio optimization of a landing page. However, what happens when we zoom out, combine them, and take a more complete approach?

AI will profoundly change how marketing campaigns are executed. With new machine-learning tools, you can create campaigns that listen and adapt automatically to audiences to improve performance. Tools can hyper-personalize the messaging using dynamic content, adapt email send times, and more. Some tools go beyond specific marketing campaigns and use machine learning to personalize and optimize the entire customer journey, in effect adjusting them for each individual person.

For automated campaign optimization, it's important that the system can automatically find and exploit the best messages through multivariate experimentation, searching for the best message option to drive click-throughs without prompting the user to unsubscribe. Tools can test anything about an electronic message including subject lines, copy or body text, design elements, graphics, and more. Campaign optimization tools perform experiments that automatically shift from lower performing towards higher performing messages. They can adapt the email send times as well to optimize the open rate.

Motiva is a company that fits this niche. Their tool creates marketing that listens and adapts automatically to audiences. This helps marketing teams save time and enhances the response performance of campaigns. David Gutelius, CEO and co-founder of Motiva, explains:

"At a high level, leveraging customer data in a deeper way creates the opportunity to uncover meaningful populations that exhibit shared content preferences. This opens up new ways to understand customers, both individually and in larger segments, as well as tailor personalized messaging experiences."

In essence, this involves learning what relationships exist, if any, between customer attribute and behavior data and their responses to the available message options in an ongoing campaign. Gutelius continues:

"By learning models that predict the likelihood of message engagement based on customer attribute and behavior data, we are automatically learning definitions of the underlying populations that are most likely interested in the associated message content. Coupled with an evolving model of message content similarity, the game changes. The possibility of continuous learning across campaigns without human intervention is within reach."

With tools like this, we can go from executing one campaign targeting a million leads, to automatically running a million campaigns in parallel, each targeting one lead with a hyper-personalized message.

BloomReach is another tool vendor in this space. They try to improve the digital experiences by optimizing the customer journey. Artificial intelligence technology is used to eliminate the guesswork from digital experience design. Data harvesting, machine learning, and intelligent analysis are used to create a personalized user journey for every individual visitor using the content available. The system also helps suggest what content is missing that would be valued by visitors, and helps companies produce only the content that provides value.

I had a conversation with Tjeerd Brenninkmeijer, EVP of EMEA at BloomReach. His take on AI in digital marketing is that smart algorithms will help marketers make better decisions instead of simply replacing them. He says the combination of human creativity and the machine's ability to process big amounts of data within a short period will be most impactful on the business. According to him, it's not likely that AI is going to take over people's jobs on a large scale. Instead, it will make people more productive and help them drive better business outcomes. I've heard the same conclusions from other industry experts as well, and I agree.

A company called Pointillist offers another customer journey optimization product that can visualize the actual paths your customers take graphically as they engage with your company across touchpoints over time. Their tool links customer behavior and metrics like revenue, profitability, churn, or customer lifetime value, and can help segment customers so you can determine an optimal engagement strategy for every individual visitor. Additionally, marketing automation system vendor Act-on now supports adaptive customer journeys, that can predict and deliver the best message, at the right time, through the ideal channel, with machine learning.

As we've seen, relationships can be improved at scale if the customer journey of each lead is personalized. We can expect most marketing automation system vendors to include AI-powered customer journey personalization in the next few years. This will be an important area for AI in marketing going forward, and those who do not adopt these strategies risk being left behind.

Cognitive Systems

While we don't yet have strong artificial intelligence that can learn new tasks completely by itself, handle tasks it isn't pre-programmed for, or have self-awareness and emotions, it appears cognitive computing may be moving in that direction. The most well-known cognitive system is probably IBM Watson, which famously won Jeopardy in 2011 over the game's best players in the world.

Cognitive systems understand unstructured data and natural language, can interact with humans in a natural way, and sift through enormous amounts of unstructured data, providing suggestions and decision support in specific fields of expertise. According to IBM, Watson augments human abilities by scaling and accelerating human expertise. In effect, it helps share experience at scale.

Cognitive systems are defined by how they understand natural text, speech, and have vision using image recognition. They use deep machine learning to learn almost everything about any topic at scale, and they can reason and provide suggestions to help people in their decision-making. Cognitive computing enables the democratization of expertise by taking the knowledge of an industry's best experts and sharing it with others. In effect, these systems are decision support tools with skills in particular topics, say cancer treatment, tax auditing, or something else entirely.

They can help share the highest levels of expertise outside the core competence centers and help make this knowledge accessible to a wider audience. For example, a cancer diagnostic decision system could be trained with the majority of the worlds combined knowledge on the matter. It can then be used by small local hospitals in rural areas or by doctors in poor countries on the other side of the world. This could improve the quality and efficiency of advanced medical treatment at a grand scale.

For our purposes, IBM Watson also brings cognitive computing to marketers, offering capabilities such as customer journey analysis, real-time personalization, surfacing marketing insights, and cognitive content management. While IBM pushes the built-in marketing capabilities of Watson, this is not the only interesting aspect of the platform. Perhaps more importantly, IBM allows developers to build their own domain-specific apps that use Watson as an AI-engine for cognitive computing. This makes it relatively simple to design advanced cognitive AI systems by building applications on top of IBM Watson.

This is what Equals3 did to create Lucy, an AI agent that can perform market research and harvest insights, provide marketing decision support, and facilitate automatic generation of buyer personas and media strategies. Other companies do the same, for example to create smart in-store digital signage or information kiosks that can adapt their content and tone of communication dependent on who uses them.

Perhaps we will see only a handful of advanced AI systems from the big vendors in the future, and all other AI tools will be built as apps on top of them. Time will tell, but it is certainly an interesting thought. With that model, any small business could build super-smart cognitive AI systems for particular niches, using AI platform technology well beyond what they could ever develop from scratch by themselves. Either way, cognitive AI might have enormous effects on the democratization of knowledge and expertise in the future, as everyone could have the world's combined knowledge on virtually any topic accessible through a simple chat or voice interface. Broadening access to these high-level tools will likely have wide-ranging implications as they develop.

Chapter Summary

We have covered some of the most exciting and prominent players and tools in the world of AI marketing, though there are many more out there. They each augment, improve, or automate common marketing tasks, without the need for the marketer to know much—if anything at all—about AI itself. Some even allow uses well beyond what most marketers could likely conceive.

With an overview of the current marketplace out of the way, let's focus on how machine learning works and how you can develop your own company-specific AI solutions that harvest insights and trigger automated decision logic, based on your own company-internal data.

BUILD YOUR OWN AI

As we have seen, there is a wide range pre-made tools on the market. However, they may not meet your company's specific needs. What if you want to leverage insights that are harvested from data that is so special to your company or industry that no commercial product is available to address the problem? This is when you need to develop your own AI software. Many businesses have already created their own machine learning solutions catered specifically to their needs.

In this chapter, I will outline why and how you can create a data-driven machine learning solution for your company. You will learn where an AI system may be useful, and the basic concepts behind how such a system is developed and works. After this overview, later chapters will go into additional detail.

How do you know if it makes sense to develop your own AI tool? Typically, this is appropriate if you want to:

- Use AI insights for data-driven marketing, or
- Use AI to improve your products or services

To develop your own AI software solution, you will have to manage your own software development projects, and later sections will touch upon that. Now, let's start by outlining how custom-designed and company-specific machine learning solutions can be beneficial.

Use AI to Trigger Marketing Campaigns

Many companies have vast amounts of domain-specific data in internal databases or from external sources. This can include customer behavior like travel or shipping patterns, yoga class attendance, media consumption, farmers' fertilization patterns, or any number of other things. Insights made from such data can drive marketing automation logic, perhaps triggering a sequence of marketing emails when a particular customer matches a specific behavioral pattern.

For example, a chain of health clubs can detect if a certain attendance pattern correlates to the member cancelling their membership a few weeks or months later. Whenever a member shows a similar pattern, marketing automation logic or manual outreach can be used to interact with them and aim to prevent the member from cancelling their membership.

In a similar manner, mobile phone network operators, on-demand video suppliers like Netflix, or other companies that offer subscription products can detect subscribers with the same behavior pattern as other customers that cancelled the subscription in the past. Trial or demo versions of software or cloud services can measure how new users are using the software. If their behavior pattern matches those of people who never bought the program, marketing or onboarding activities can be added to encourage them to purchase it.

Retail chains already monitor purchase patterns closely and use machine learning algorithms to try to draw insights from this information, promoting products they think will interest each customer based on their previous purchase patterns. We can find any number of situations where data that are already available can be used to drive personalized and context-specific marketing automation logic, thus providing highly relevant marketing outreach.

To do things like this, you can build a machine learning system that harvests insights from the data you have, and then lets those insights trigger relevant marketing automation workflows (which we discuss in Appendix 1). This could include sending a sequence of applicable nurturing or campaign emails to those who match the situation you want to detect and leverage.

Use AI in Software or Service Businesses

While it may be tempting to analyze existing data for insights that can drive automatic and context-specific marketing activities as outlined above, this is not the only way custom-developed machine learning software can be used. In fact, companies can benefit from this in many other ways too.

Cloud software suppliers can integrate voice control to their solutions relatively easily using Amazon Alexa. You can, for example, speak to digital logistics software like LogTrade and ask it to order—or check the status of—parcel shipments using voice commands. While voice control using Amazon Alexa doesn't require the system's developer to come up with their own AI-based voice recognition software (they piggyback on Alexa for this), it still improves the product through its use of AI.

Other organizations can leverage AI to come up with completely new products or services built around AI-based insights. Companies in the finance industry, for example, can sell services that use stock market trading robots, or offer robot-driven equity funds. Insurance companies can use machine learning for risk assessment. The list goes on. Most of the marketing tools mentioned so far in this book belong to this category of AI-based software products, as they are created for the sole purpose of making a software business out of AI-based insights.

Machine learning can also be used to improve the behavior or capabilities of existing software, which wasn't initially created to commercialize AI. Consider for example personalized send times of some email marketing software, or predictive lead scoring in some CRM or marketing automation software. In those cases, such AI-based functionalities are often added to the core product well after it is launched.

Developers of other types of software can find many other ways to integrate AI in a similar manner, using predictive analytics or machine learning to improve a program's behavior or user experience. Suppliers of accounting software now look for AI to implement automated book keeping, for example. If you are in the software business, it is likely your product can benefit from injecting machine learning into it, and if you are in the service business—not offering software to your customers—you may still be in luck.

You can use home-grown machine learning solutions to aid or optimize the internal work within your organization on several fronts. Take companies that sell used cars or real-estate properties, for example. In these markets, it is hard to predict the right price, since no identical products are available for comparison. Using machine learning, such companies could develop software tools that are used in-house to help predict the correct selling price. Risk assessment inside insurance companies is another example. If you are in the trucking or logistics industry, perhaps you could gather insights on how certain companies ship their goods. Understanding these patterns may have a business value, and some might trigger highly targeted and personalized marketing campaigns based on the transport flow of the customers.

As we have seen, there is no shortage of examples where AI can be used to improve software or service products. Now, let's look at how the physical products can be improved by AI too.

Use AI in Physical Products

While many companies are still struggling to enter the world of traditional marketing automation and data-driven marketing, state-of-the-art marketing departments are looking at AI for the future, as we have already discussed. The fact that you are reading this book indicates you are an early adopter, eager to stay ahead of your competition by leveraging the best technologies out there.

All of this is incredible, but in my opinion, AI in marketing is just an intermediate step. The next big thing in marketing, after AI, will be the Internet of things, or IoT. This is where almost all machines, instruments, and devices are connected to the Internet. McKinsey even expects there will be a trillion Internet-connected devices by 2025.[13]

This can include nearly anything electronic, including bathroom scales, industrial sensors and machinery, washing machines, cars, heating systems, burglar alarms, windmill farms, and the like. For more on IoT and how it will change the world, read my book, *The Internet of Things – The Next Industrial Revolution Has Begun*, available on Amazon.[14]

What do Internet-connected machines have to do with marketing? A lot, at least if you look into the crystal ball and try to understand the future. AI-driven marketing relies upon one thing: the availability of data, and lots of it.

So far, this book has covered AI-analysis built on top of data related to how people behave. But what happens when a trillion or so machines

---

13   "No Ordinary Disruption," McKinsey & Company, 13 April 2015. Via LinkedIn: *https://www.slideshare.net/McKinseyCompany/no-ordinary-disruption-the-four-forces*

14   *https://www.amazon.com/Internet-Things-Industrial-Revolution-predictive-ebook/dp/ B077RLMGSW*

become Internet connected, generating oceans of data about how they are used? If we can collect this data, and find valuable business insights from it, we can use it to trigger marketing automation logic that initiates marketing activities towards different people and companies, based on readings and insights from how their machines and devices are used and operate. What a revolution to the marketing industry that will be!

With vibration and heat sensors on industrial machines, predictive analytics and machine learning can be used to detect when a machine is about to break down, perhaps weeks in advance. If these insights are integrated into a marketing automation system, it can send automatic marketing emails offering spare parts or service visits to prevent the machine from malfunctioning in the first place, thus minimizing downtime and possibly reducing the cost of the repair. This monitoring and reporting will be fully autonomous, without any manual intervention at all.

Perhaps weight loss clubs put an Internet-connected bathroom scale in the home of their members. When the machine-learning algorithms detect a pattern of someone who matches those of other people who have gained weight one month later, the daily personalized recipes or training schedule could be adjusted automatically to prevent the weight increase from happening. Perhaps new recipes are emailed as a consequence, or pushed to a smartphone app. The automated food delivery service from your grocery store might adapt the deliveries accordingly as well.

The possibilities are almost endless, and only imagination limits what types of automated marketing outreach can be done when data from physical products can be analyzed and integrated into your marketing machinery. AI could be used to improve the products themselves as well. Medical X-ray machines could use image recognition to detect cancer from scans automatically, or a farmer's tractors could use AI to optimize the amount of irrigation or fertilizers needed on different parts of the field, thus saving money and improving yield.

For your company, this will add more value to product offerings, possibly justifying a price increase or at least improving competitiveness. In addition to using AI to improve your marketing, you may consider how your product portfolio and product roadmap can be improved by adding AI capabilities to the products themselves. These systems promise a world of possibilities for both new products and internal processes.

The Structure of a Machine Learning System

So you have decided to develop your own custom AI software to improve your marketing, or the products and services themselves. Now, how do you actually do it? This section will provide an overview of the process, and later, we'll look at it in more detail.

To simplify this section, let's assume we have a machine learning algorithm we want to use, without worrying about which one it is or how it works. This makes it easier to understand how you would go about developing your own AI software.

First, we need to remember that machine learning solutions are trained from historical data. In other words, the software behavior is derived from data we already have. Hence, we will likely need a great deal of historical data and a data scientist that knows how to build a machine learning system from it. Before we continue, this data must be cleaned and normalized. For example, out-of-range values will be set to the minimum or maximum allowed value or removed; missing values may be replaced by the average value from nearby data points; and temperature values are standardized to Celsius or Fahrenheit, but not both. With the data in better shape, a data scientist can start to make experiments, trying to find patterns in the data that correlate to the outcome we want to detect and predict.

When the data scientist has found a pattern that signals the situation we want to predict (for example, what website behavior correlates to the customer defecting soon), he or she continues by researching which specific algorithm performs best, and then implements it as a prediction model. This prediction model can then make predictions from future new data, for example to determine if a customer is likely to churn soon. The model implementation is often deployed on a readymade machine learning platform, often a cloud service from companies like Microsoft, Amazon, or Google. Using such a platform, the prediction model is exposed (or published) to the world in the form of a web service that can make the desired predictions.

To use the prediction model, some application software (typically a smartphone app, a cloud software solution, or a PC application) consumes the predictions by sending new data to the prediction model and asking for the result. For example, "Will this customer stop buying soon?" The prediction model may reply with, "Yes, to a 91% likelihood." It is thus common to separate the actual application software that solves a domain-specific problem (like email sending or a CRM system) from the prediction module (which may determine the optimal send-time for each email recipient, or the lead score of someone in the CRM database).

As the prediction model is exposed to new data over time, it can retrain itself to adjust for changes in the environment. Perhaps a bank detects which new credit card transactions have been fraudulent and feeds this information into the algorithm for daily re-training, making the fraud detection model adapt to changes in the outside world. The concept can be illustrated like this:

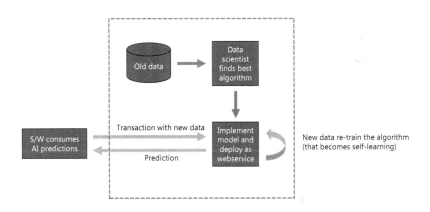

To conclude this, we've seen how data scientists use historical data and machine learning algorithms to develop a prediction model that knows how to make predictions from new data in the future. Some kind of application software sends new data to the prediction model and gets predictions in return that can be used to build new software functionality. The prediction model can be retrained once new data is available to make it adapt its prediction behavior to changing conditions.

Chapter Summary

In this chapter, we explored how custom-designed machine-learning solutions can be useful to many companies. They implement data-driven approaches to trigger marketing automation campaigns, can be used in software or service businesses, and even be integrated in your physical products to add value. With this broad view out of the way, let's dive a bit deeper into the data science involved.

BIG DATA

As mentioned in the introduction, artificial intelligence can be thought of as being based on three cornerstone technologies. The first, big data, is about finding patterns and correlations in historical data to uncover insights that are useful for some purpose. With predictive analytics, we create algorithms that can detect such patterns in future unknown data, thus predicting outcomes and valuable facts from within it. Finally, machine learning adds a feedback loop in which the prediction algorithm is re-trained automatically as new data is added over time to make the predictions adapt as the environment changes. We'll cover each of these, but let's start with big data.

What is Big Data?

Big data is a collection of information that is so large it doesn't fit into traditional databases, and cannot be processed by a single computer. It might also be changing too fast, or it may be in an unstructured format not suited for processing in a traditional database. The data often come from a variety of sources, for example traditional databases, server log files, social media engagement, website visits and page views, image/sound/video-analytics, website or email copy, or virtually anything else.

To find valuable insights from such vast amounts of unorganized data, we must process it in a way traditional database systems can't. Big data is about finding useful insights that were previously not possible to extract by finding undetected patterns and relationships. It has only recently become both affordable and feasible to analyze enormous sets of data, which couldn't be done in the past due to the sheer size or the computing power required to do it.

A key aspect of big data is that it only works when there is enough of it; these methods will generally not work well on small data sets. However, what constitutes enough data depends on the problem at hand. You can gain new insights if you analyze three thousand parameters instead of three, and if you do it every second instead of once per day. More data often outweighs better algorithms with less data. In short, big data enables us to analyze all available data points instead of just a few samples. With the previous technological limitations, a limited set of samples had to be used to reduce the computational load. Consequently, many useful patterns and correlations could not be found. This is no longer a problem, and all available data can now be included in the analysis.

A problem is that big data is often unstructured and messy. As it comes from a variety of sources, its quality might vary. However, larger volumes enable us to accept reduced quality because size compensates for accuracy. With much more data, even if it is of lower quality, we can detect trends and relationships that can't be found with smaller samples. Often, understanding the general pattern and revealing a trend is more important than having precise information on the exact details.

But how are the insights found? To discover patters in data, scientists and programmers use statistical analysis and data mining algorithms that detect correlations. Correlation is the statistical relationship between different data values. If two data values have a strong relationship, one value is likely to change when the other does. Finding correlations in data is the centerpiece of big data analysis. This is how we can know certain website or purchase behavior patterns can be a signal of churn, for example. This can be done if there is a correlation between certain digital footprint patterns and churn in historical data. In short, big data is about finding correlations between aspects of a data set—links or relationships hidden in the vast sea of information that cannot be detected by a human.

With big data, you will know what insights was found, but not why they occurred. Knowing the "what" but not the "why" can be a difficult situation to accept for some people. Nevertheless, sufficient data volumes can help make conclusions even if no explanation is available. If we can detect that fewer people die from a particular disease if they adhere to a specific diet, it might be so valuable that understanding why the correlation exists is of secondary importance. As big data comes into widespread use, we will get to know the world in ways we haven't seen before.

Data is the New Currency

Large volumes of raw data may have a significant commercial value. Even if it doesn't have an obvious value right now, it may in the future, so many systems are collecting as much data as possible at all times. Who knows what valuable insights we might find later? We might find insights that save money, improve operational efficiency, or increase customer satisfaction. Without that data, though, there can be no insights or advancement.

We can also use big data to create new products and even new companies. Take Google as an example. They can sell valuable insights found from mining search query data and offer that knowledge as a service. In fact, their entire business model is based on selling ad space that relates to certain search keywords. Not all companies will have their own data to use, but others will make a living from selling the data they collect, or insights harvested from it. Having access to large amounts of data will have a major business value going forward. This is why some say that data is the new currency—or the new oil, since it must be refined to become useful.

Democratization of Supercomputing

While big data analysis has been feasible for government organizations and some companies for a few years, it has historically been quite expensive. Huge companies like Google and Walmart were early adopters, as can be expected. But we now see the democratization of big data in technical developments combined with cheap cloud-based services from companies like Microsoft or Amazon that enable small companies to build their own big data systems. This enables them to gather new insights, acquire new knowledge, and even build new data-based products.

When speaking of big data, we often discuss the three V's: the Volume (data size), the Velocity (speed of the data flow), and the Variety (how unstructured the information is). Previously, it was reasonably easy to get two out of the three, but until recently, it has been very expensive to get all three at the same time. This is changing. Big data has made affordable commercial supercomputing a reality. Data mining and data processing can now be performed at scale at relatively low cost, often on distributed systems and parallel processing using hundreds or even thousands of computers at the same time.

While advanced computing hardware can be impressive, one new software package made big data possible in wider circles. This software platform is Apache Hadoop, the most popular solution for big data processing.

Hadoop

Apache Hadoop was the first commercially affordable supercomputing platform for big data analysis. The software is open-source, thus free of charge. Originally, Hadoop was developed by Doug Cutting and Mike Cafarella at Yahoo! in 2005, and it is considered a significant contributor to the growth of big data at large. Hadoop is a software framework for distributed storage and processing of very large data sets—up to thousands or millions of gigabytes of data. In short, it can compute and analyze huge amounts of unstructured data in a highly efficient manner.

It does this thanks to a job scheduler that distributes the work on many computers sharing complex tasks. Hadoop assumes all computers in the computational cluster can fail, and its software features are able to recover from those errors. This helps provide a high-availability service even when thousands of computers—which all might fail at one point or another—are thrown at a massive task. By using software that can recover from hardware failures, expensive high-reliability computer clusters are no longer necessary. Instead, Hadoop can use cheap standard computers, thus reducing cost. The advantage is that it can make a query over a huge dataset and split it into smaller parts that can be analyzed on many computers in parallel.

Hadoop is the de-facto standard for big data analysis, but how can you use this free software in your company? It's certainly possible to install it on your own computers manually, but it might be simpler to use a readymade pre-packaged Hadoop distribution from one of the available vendors. However, you may want to go a different route: You can now rent access to a cloud-based big data platform from many hosting companies like Amazon or Microsoft. With such a solution, you can get started right away.

The key takeaway here is that big data is now democratized, and almost anyone can afford it—even small companies. There's no longer a need to have your own data center with massive server farms. A hosting supplier and a credit card will get you going immediately, provided you have data to analyze and the required skills. Many companies even hire dedicated data scientists to help them get the most out of these systems. Let's look a little more at what these people do.

Data Scientists

We have looked at many examples of how data analysis can address a wide variety of marketing problems. The force behind these tools, though, is built around data scientists. Data science is an interdisciplinary field that focuses on finding ways to pull insights from data.

Among other things, data scientists build systems for analysis using big data. They pull from diverse backgrounds with cross-domain knowledge in math, statistics, analytics, software development, and computer science. Data scientists commonly use a programming language called R to analyze vast amounts of data. This domain-specific language was developed by Ross Ihaka and Robert Gentleman from the University of Auckland in New Zealand, and is optimized for statistical computing and data mining. Python is also a common programming language in AI, but it is more often used by the solutions developers (programmers) rather than the algorithm developers (data scientists).

Data scientists need to understand what insights have value to the organization. To do this, they must have strong logical thinking skills to find ways to process the data before experiments determine what algorithms to implement. They must also be able to communicate the insights found in data in a simplified way so that managers can understand and are comfortable using them in their decision-making. We'll learn more about this process below.

Chapter Summary

Big data and related data mining software solutions provide the statistical foundation used to find correlations in data patterns and expose the business insights we want to find and predict. Having access to data is becoming increasingly important, and data scientists use sophisticated methods to find these correlations. The required technology is now available at relatively low cost using cloud services you can rent and get started with right away. Armed with that foundation, let's move from finding facts and insights from old data to unlocking the future using predictive analytics and machine learning.

PREDICTIVE ANALYTICS AND MACHINE LEARNING

With an understanding of big data and the detection of valuable patterns and correlations in historical data, let's turn to predictions and machine learning. First, we need to understand the basics of software development. Traditionally, software programs have used input data to produce output data, like this:

INPUT DATA + PROGRAM => OUTPUT DATA

Software developers would carefully craft the program by manually developing thousands or millions of lines of code. Once developed, the program was fixed and generally couldn't adapt its behavior unless developers rewrote it and deployed a new version. For example, grammar-checking software wouldn't improve its language capabilities unless programmers wrote a better algorithm and updated the software to use it.

With machine learning, this well-established concept is turned upside down. Instead, the software behavior is generated from historical data. Now, the process looks like this:

INPUT DATA + OUTPUT DATA => PROGRAM

In other words, the software behavior is derived—or trained—from old data. As new data becomes available, the algorithm can simply be regenerated—or retrained—from the updated dataset, thus adapting its behavior to changes in the environment. When this process happens repeatedly, the software effectively becomes self-learning and self-adapting. This is the foundational principle of machine learning.

For example, a grammar-checking algorithm based on machine learning is not written as software code. Rather, it is trained to know correct grammar by analyzing the patterns in a large set of text documents that are known to be free of major errors, such as tens of thousands of books. A large collection of training data like this is called a corpus.

Any new text being grammar-checked is considered to have grammatical errors if it doesn't match the patterns of those training texts. If more training data becomes available, say a new corpus with a few thousand extra books, the grammar-checking algorithm can simply be re-generated by taking the new material into account. It can then offer improved grammar-checking capabilities without programmers having to write better software algorithms. If this is done continuously—say the model is retrained every time a new book is launched on Amazon—we get a truly self-learning system that knows how to improve its grammar checking automatically.

The importance of being able to generate and re-generate software logic automatically from data cannot be underestimated. This is what powers AI, and it will create the most disruptive force the world has seen to date. Since the consequences of this capability are so far-reaching, let's dig into some details. To start with, it is valuable to understand how different algorithms are classified by what they do or how they are trained. I touched upon this in the introduction, but let's go through this again in some more detail.

Types of Models

AI can be used to solve such a wide variety of problems in business and marketing, and several types of prediction algorithms can be used for different types of problems. Let's look at four types.

With binary classification algorithms, we are looking to determine if something is likely to be true or false, such as if a customer is likely to stop purchasing from us or if a lead is a good fit for a certain product. Put another way, binary classification algorithms can predict the outcome when there are only two possible alternatives.

The second type is multi-class classification algorithms. These can predict which out of a number of predefined possibilities is most likely, for example if a person is most likely to prefer red wine, white wine, or sparking wine, or if a face in a social media photograph is most likely happy, sad, or angry.

While binary or multi-class classification algorithms attempt to predict the most likely value from a small set of predefined values, regression algorithms try to predict a numeric value in any range, such as the most likely selling price of a home or the number of days before a customer is likely to make the next purchase.

With clustering algorithms, we can group certain data points that are similar to each other in some way to create a set of categories, or to place pieces of information in different buckets based on some type of similarity. Clustering analyses can be used for automatic segmentation of customers and for the creation of look-alike audiences, for example.

With these types of AI algorithms, we can build predictive or prescriptive marketing systems that help automate useful tasks. In fact, many AI-based solutions use not only one, but a combination of many types of AI algorithms to build more complex problem-solving capabilities. In the next chapter, we'll look at these in more detail, including how some common algorithms work and why one type may be better suited for a certain kind of problem.

Types of Learning

Different machine-learning algorithms are used to build software tools that are available on the market today, and most belong to one of the model types we described. However, in addition to classifying algorithms by what they do, they can also be sorted by how they learn. Let's look at the three broad categories of learning.

Supervised learning algorithms are often used for classification and regression problems. With these, you train the model from historical data. In short, you have access to the input data and the outcomes from old data. That is used to teach the model the most likely outcome for various patterns of input attribute values. For new unknown data, the algorithm can then predict the most likely outcome based on the input attribute patterns. Credit-card fraud detection is a good example. Many old credit card transactions are used to teach the model, some of which are known to be fraudulent. Then, when future behavior is noted to follow similar patterns, the fraud can be flagged and prevented.

Unsupervised learning algorithms are designed to detect insights in data where the desired outcome is unknown. Effectively, you don't know exactly what you are looking for, as with automated customer segmentation. Here, we don't know what similarities will be found among the customers, and the software helps create those classifications. Rather than relying on gut feeling, an unsupervised algorithm can learn from the data and present the customer segmentation you actually have. In effect, the data will tell you what is going on.

The final group is reinforcement learning algorithms. These are inspired by behavioral psychology and are taught by providing a feedback loop that let the algorithm know if a previous decision was a good or a bad one. In effect, the model is rewarded for good decisions and punished for bad ones as it tries different approaches using trial and error. Tools performing automated conversion ratio optimization are candidates for reinforcement learning, for example. As the tool adjust the landing page design, the model learns what changes improved the conversion rate and which didn't, and adjusts accordingly for future decisions.

With a basic understanding of what different types of algorithms do, and how they learn, let's move on to discussing how to build and use these systems.

Work Process

The most time-consuming tasks of a machine learning project are finding the right data, importing it, and cleaning it for successful use. Since the algorithms get more precise if trained on large volumes of data, this preparation can be a major task. The initial step is to identify and find the data to be imported. It can come from any source, including traditional well-structured databases, images, log files, or other places. It must all be merged into the same system to enable a coherent analysis.

Thereafter, the data must be massaged into better shape, for example, by deleting incorrect data fields, filling in void data fields with the average value of nearby data points, or by setting out-of-range values to acceptable minimum or maximum values. You may need to do some pre-processing calculations to complete this step as well. You may need to scale data points to a normalized number, for example by changing all monetary values to the same currency, or aligning date formats from different countries. Skipping this step will lead to inferior algorithm performance; in other words, poor predictions.

With the data properly imported and cleaned, the data scientist will try many different machine learning algorithms and datasets to find a solution that produces the most precise behavior—meaning predictions of high accuracy. When machine learning models are trained to make predictions from data, they often use input attributes and the known outcome in historical data. Think of this historical data as a two-dimensional matrix. The table below illustrates how certain types of credit card transactions were known to be fraudulent.

Historical data

	Input attributes					Outcome
Transaction	Country	Amount	Sex	Time	...	Fraudulent?
1	US	100	Male	9:23	...	Yes
2	UK	200	Female	23:12	...	No
3	US	125	Male	0:45	...	No
4	US	400	Male	14:34	...	No
5	CA	240	Female	11:00	...	No
...	...	...	...	...	...	...

When a prediction algorithm is trained, it learns from the known outcome (the rightmost column) for different patterns of input attribute data (all other columns). So, part of the work process for the data scientist is to find algorithms that can accurately detect the outcome based on a set if input attributes. To find the most precise prediction algorithm, many alternative algorithms must be tested and compared with each other for accuracy.

Every repetition of this task is called an experiment, in which the data scientist tries different ways to find the best solution. The result of every experiment is a candidate model. Each candidate model must be tested such that it can be compared to other candidate models for prediction accuracy. Of course, we can't test a new algorithm on future data that does not exist yet, and we can't test it using the data its behavior is derived from, as it would by definition make perfect predictions.

This problem is easily solved by not using all the historical data to train the model during an experiment. Instead, use 70% of the historical data for training the model (we call this the training data), and keep the remaining 30% (which we call the testing data) to use for testing the model's performance.

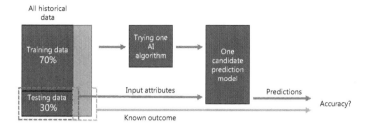

In this way, we can test the precision of the algorithm versus known data from which it wasn't derived. Just like in the table above, the leftmost columns in the "All historical data" section of the illustration above represents the input attributes, and the rightmost column represents the known outcome for the corresponding input attributes in the historical data.

With each candidate model from all the experiments at hand, the one that performs best—i.e. gives the most accurate predictions—is selected for deployment and commercial use. So far, the data scientist has worked only in the "laboratory," far from actual software implementations and live data used to make predictions in production use. Now, the winning algorithm has to be translated into software code that can actually make the predictions on live production data. At this point, theoretical statistics are replaced by software development to build a solution that can be deployed for commercial use.

The key takeaway here is that the machine learning algorithms use historical data to create a prediction model, which detects the valuable pattern in future unseen data. The actual prediction model runs as software code and is the solution to the problem being solved. They are integrated into the software application that consumes the predictions, while the machine learning algorithms are only used for the training of the prediction models.

Finally, it is worth noting that prediction models usually do not provide an exact answer to a question, for example, if a customer will defect or not. Instead, the prediction algorithms usually return a probability factor in the range of 0-100%. So, instead of getting a clear answer if a particular customer will defect, you might get a predicted likelihood of 92%.

Bias

One of the advantages of predictive analytics and machine learning is they help make data-driven decisions. If the decisions are truly data-driven, they are free from any unfairness introduced by human emotions and bias, such as gender, sexual, religious or ethnic prejudices. In theory, data-driven decision-making is a great equalizer, removing unfair bias and making all decisions objective and free of discrimination. In practice, this may not always be the case.

AI systems are only as good as the data you give to them. If the training set itself is skewed, so is the result. If an AI algorithm is trained on data that, for example, under- or over-represents a certain group, then the resulting algorithm might be biased as well. The developer of the system is likely not even aware of this fact. This comes back to a common saying among software developers: "garbage in, garbage out." Take a bank's loan granting system as an example. A woman might be refused a loan because she is considered a greater credit risk than a man with otherwise similar financial attributes. This decision may at least partly be deduced from the average income levels, which might be lower for women at large, and this could place this particular woman at a disadvantage when applying for a loan.

An infamous example of bias is Google's image recognition software, which tagged two black people as gorillas in 2015. On June 28, 2015, the Google Photo app repeatedly tagged computer programmer Jacky Alciné and his girlfriend as gorillas, thus showing racist bias. This happened because the image recognition algorithm was trained with data sets containing too few people of color. A Google manager, Yonatan Zunger, quickly apologized for the feature. Google attempted to fix the algorithm, but ultimately removed the gorilla label altogether and as of May 2018, the system has not been updated sufficiently to reintroduce it.

Since the algorithms learn from the data we train them with, any bias in the training data might end up as a biased algorithm. This may not only be unethical, but can be illegal as well, since it creates discrimination. It isn't easy to remove bias from all AI-based automated decision making, as we aren't even aware of it most of the time. Data scientists will have to worry a lot more about bias in the future to keep their companies out of trouble. One way of addressing this problem is to ensure algorithms are taught by sufficient amounts of data, and that the data set is fully representative of the problem being solved. Both data quality and data quantity are important here, but bias is and will probably remain a problem for quite some time. Later, we will go into more detail on legal and ethical matters related to autonomous decision making with AI.

Chapter Summary

Now that we have the basics of predictive analytics and machine learning under our belts, it's time for an overview of how some actual algorithms used in AI software work. Even if you aren't interested in the mathematical details, it will be valuable to get an overview of how it all works. It isn't smoke and mirrors, after all.

After the next chapter, we'll continue our discussion with a look at how you can implement and deploy your own AI solution, how AI may disrupt your job or company, which other technologies might disrupt the marketing industry after AI, and how AI is set to change society as a whole. But first, let's dive into the world of data science to learn more about the algorithms that power these systems.

AI ALGORITHMS

With an overview of the process out of the way, let's take a quick detour into the world of the data scientists. This chapter will outline some of the more popular AI algorithms, but it will do so on a popular-science level that anyone will understand. Don't worry, you won't see any formulas filled with Greek symbols.

The chapter is intended to provide a basic look at what really drives AI-based marketing. Understanding the information from this chapter is by no means necessary to use AI in your marketing department, but I have included it for completeness and to add some meat to the bones of the topic. Knowledge is rarely a burden.

Just remember that algorithms are commonly classified by how they learn:

- Supervised learning (trained by historical data)
- Unsupervised learning (insights are found in the data)
- Reinforcement learning (trained by positive or negative experiences)

They are also divided by what they do:

- Classification algorithms (predict one of several predefined possibilities)
- Regression algorithms (predict a numeric value in any range)
- Clustering algorithms (predict group similarity)

There are a large number of different algorithms, all suited for different types of problems. This book will not outline them all but we mention a few and explain what they do. These algorithms are covered:

- Regression
  - Simple linear regression
  - Multiple linear regression
  - Logistic regression

- Classification
  - Decision Trees
  - K-Nearest Neighbors
  - Naïve Bayes
  - Neural networks

- Clustering
  - K-Means
  - DBSCAN
  - Agglomerative

With that said, I will leave the rest of this chapter to my friend Martin Wass, who is a skilled data scientist and statistician. Without further ado, here is his pop-sci explanation of data science and some of the more common algorithms used in predictive marketing and machine learning.

Data Science and Technical Terms

In the field of data science, there can be an overwhelming number of technical terms. Some are hard to get your head around, even for analysts! However, most of them are easily understood after some basic concepts are explained.

The fundamental focus of all data analysis is to study how variables are related to each other and how this relationship can be leveraged to predict outcomes. Let's start at the beginning: What is a variable? What does it mean for two variables to have a relationship? What is an observation in data science?

Before diving in to the more data-orientated terms, let's consider the term 'observation'. When we collect data for analysis in marketing, we observe how our customers behave. We will structure our collected data so the information about one customer has its own row where the characteristics (or attributes) are in different columns. Because every row in our data contains information about a single observed customer, every row is called an observation. To put it in one sentence, one observed customer equals one observation. Take a look back at the table in the Work Process section above to get a sense of how this is organized.

A variable contains information about one attribute of all the observations (customers) being studied, described by one column in the table. If we want to study how fast a sports car can round a track, we will collect data about many separate cars driving that track, or maybe even data about cars on other similar tracks. Since not all sports cars are exactly the same, we cannot simply measure the time it takes for one car to do the loop. We also want to collect data about which type of tires the cars used, what kind of engine they have, and more. These are attributes of each individual car, and for our purposes, they are the variables we use when trying to explain how long it takes a car to cover the track.

A relationship between variables is how they are associated with each other. A sports car's time around the track will be dependent on which engine it uses, for example. This means there is a relationship between the time it takes to finish the track and the engine variable. When analyzing the relationship between variables, we aim to set up models based on the data we have collected. We use those models to explain the relationship between variables in more detail. Simply put, a model is like a summary of how variables affect an outcome.

Consider a connect-the-dot exercise for kids. Each dot is a variable, and the lines children draw between them are the relationships. The model, then, is the shape that begins to emerge. As more dots are connected, the clearer the image becomes, and the more easily we can predict what the drawing represents. The model changes if dots are closer or farther apart, or grouped in different ways. Understanding the relationships between variables (dots) then helps us to explain them or even predict what will happen next. Obviously, this is a simplification and real modeling is far more complex; however, it is sufficient for our needs here.

Models can take many forms and can be used for predicting an outcome or to provide context and understanding of current data. When making a model, the variables used are classed as either dependent or independent. These terms are most often used when studying statistics, but you might hear other terms used for the same concepts. For example, in machine learning, we often call them output variables and input variables. Let's look at what some of these mean.

As the terms indicate, a dependent variable relies on or is tied to some other variable. This means that they change if one or more other variables change. Take business revenue, for example, which is dependent on number of sold units.

The opposite of dependent is independent. Just as it sounds, it is not tied to other variables. Changes in an independent variable can trigger a change in a dependent variable, but the reverse is not true. For example, if wrinkles are dependent on time passing, then time is the independent variable that can be used to explain wrinkles. However, time will not stop passing just because you don't get wrinkles. Therefore, a dependent (or output) variable can be explained or predicted using a set of independent (or input) variables. Which variables are classed as dependent or independent is decided based on the assumptions used to create the model.

Another common term in the world of data science is 'outlier,' which is an extreme observation. If you score a hole in one when playing golf, it probably doesn't reflect how you normally play. Therefore, a hole in one is an outlier to the other normal results. We may not want to take this score into account when trying to predict what score you will get when playing golf next time because it would cause the prediction to be lower than what could be expected normally, and therefore cause the prediction to be less accurate. Similarly, you probably don't want to include outliers when studying sales metrics. If a news story covers one of your products, resulting in a big but temporary jump in sales, that should be treated as an anomaly rather than what could normally be assumed in other years.

The last important term to understand is overfitting. This is defined as an analysis that corresponds too closely to a set of data, and avoiding this is one of the hardest and most crucial things in machine learning. Why would it be bad to have a model fit the data too closely? The issue is that when a model is created to explain data, it is trained using a selected set of data points. If the model fits that too closely, it's unlikely to also work when a new, larger set of data is introduced. Errors in our predictions are reduced by using a more complex model (one that can describe more aspects of the relationships between variables), but as the complexity increases, the model risks becoming less and less general. This can cause predictions based on new observations to be wrong. We'll come back to this topic a little later.

In the rest of this chapter, we will look at three groups of algorithms and explain how they work. In each group, we cover several types of algorithms that can be used for different tasks.

Regression

Now that we understand different types of variables, let's look at some ways they can relate to each other, and how that can help us understand sets of data.

The first and more straightforward group of algorithms use regression. This is a way of looking at the relationship between variables and can predict the dependent variable based on known values of the independent variables. For example, if we know that a customer is a woman with a high salary (independent variables), then we can predict how much she might spend on certain items (dependent variable). Stick with me here—it's not as complicated as it sounds. Let's break it down a little.

Simple Linear Regression

Simple linear regression is a method of predicting one value if we know the other value. While it's often too simple to use in real life data science, it's an important stepping stone to understanding the more complex algorithms we discuss later. This method assumes that the relationship between the dependent and the independent variable is linear, meaning that it can be illustrated as a straight line. Imagine climbing a mountain 1000 feet high with a constant grade or steepness. There is a linear relationship between the time you have spent walking and your elevation, assuming you walk at a constant speed. Therefore, if we know the time spent walking, we can predict the elevation that will be reached.

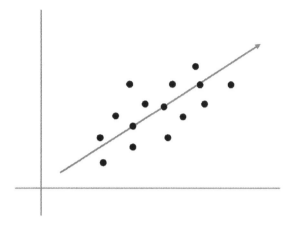

Let's look at another example. Assume that the figure above illustrates work experience in years on the horizontal line (x-axis) and salary on the vertical line (y-axis). Since a person's work experience is constantly growing, it is an independent variable. Conversely, salary is tied to work experience, so it is a dependent variable. Each point on the graph is a person's salary at a specific time. The data points vary as they work in different positions, but there is a linear relationship between the two, where salary increases with the number of years of experience.

Simple linear regression summarizes the relationship between one dependent and one independent variables by fitting a line through the scattered observations. This is called a regression line. This allows us to interpret how much the dependent variable will increase or decrease if the independent variable changes or predict the dependent variable if only knowing the value of the independent variable. In other words, by using a model to understand all the data points, we can extrapolate where your salary is expected to be after a certain number of years.

When fitting the line through the data points, the goal is to explain variations in the dependent variable as much as possible. In other words, we try to minimize the distance between the data points and the fitted line. This is why we have to handle outliers. If someone starts with an extremely high salary with only one year of experience, it would flatten out the slope of the line and reduce the model's accuracy. This is because it would be skewed by the extremely high salary and short work experience, which is an uncommon exception in a group of otherwise normal data points.

The advantage of linear regression is that it is easy to understand. This model is also easily updated with new data.

However, linear regression also has some disadvantages. Because of the simplicity, it can create problems when the assumption of a linear relationship is incorrect. It's possible to change the variables to meet the restrictions of a linear relationship, but this complicates the otherwise simple interpretation of the results. Linear regression is useful, but it also risks over simplification. As mentioned, another disadvantage is that the linear model is sensitive to extreme observations (outliers) that may not be appropriate to take into account when trying to explain a larger data set.

To turn a prediction model based on linear regression into a continuously learning and adaptive prediction system, it must import an updated data set and re-generate the regression line, taking the new data into account. If the updated data set includes points that cause the new regression line to have a different slope, the prediction model will give different predictions. If this retraining process is repeated continuously as new data points become available, the model will change its behavior (predictions), thus creating a learning machine.

Where do we go from here? Let's make things a little more complex to help us deal with bigger and more varied sets of data.

Multiple Linear Regression

Linear regression models containing more than one independent variable are called multiple linear regression models. For example, your salary may be dependent on both the type of university degree you have and the number of years you have worked, not just the years alone. Multiple linear regression is useful when seeking to discover the relationship between a set of independent variables and a continuous dependent variable, which are variables that can take any numeric value (like salary, revenue, etc.).

Just like simple linear regression, this approach assumes that there is a linear relationship between the variables. However, instead of having a linear relationship between the dependent variable and *one* independent variable, this model allows relationships with *multiple* independent variables. Let's consider the mountain climber again. We know that there is a linear relationship between the time a person has spent walking and their elevation. We can also assume that a person's height is part of that relationship because taller people go faster with a longer stride. Therefore, the dependent variable—elevation—is dependent on both the amount of time spent hiking and the length of the person's stride.

With three variables in the model, it uses a broader collection of information, and if graphed, it becomes three dimensional. Just like simple linear regression, this model allows you to interpret and explain how changes in the independent variables will affect the dependent variable in an easily accessible manner. This could be useful when wondering how different customer attributes are likely to affect how much they are spending or to predict how much a product will sell based on how much is spent on advertising and what channel is used to reach out to customers.

Multiple linear regression is like simple linear regression in that they are both easy to understand. In the real world, this is useful in supporting business decisions or explaining the effects of a particular course of action. It also allows for quick and easy predictions based on data already collected.

However, this simplicity can create some difficulties. Data scientists often change the way variables are presented by using equations to alter their value. This helps fit variables into the model, but too much manipulation of the data can weaken the model's viability and complicate our interpretation of it.

Although a data scientist can manipulate variables to achieve a linear relationship, that may not be enough to explain the data properly. Many real life problems are more complex than a linear relationship can relay, which means the model may be missing important information. However, this type of model is a powerful way to interpret information when used correctly. Now, let's look at another type of regression, used for a different type of task.

Logistic Regression

Logistic regression is similar to simple linear regression, but it is used to predict the outcome when there are only two options. For example, data about a customer are used to predict if he or she is going to buy your product or not. The likelihood of either option is calculated, and the customer is classified into the category with the highest probability, as either likely to buy, or not likely to buy.

The relationship between the variables is not presented by how much one will change if the other does, like in linear regression. Instead, the relationship is measured by the chance of belonging to the group who is likely to buy, as presented by an odds ratio.

Let's look at another example. Say you are studying how customers respond to a campaign related to their personal characteristics. This model allows you to interpret if a customer with a certain characteristics increases or decreases the chance of getting a good response. For example, it can determine if targeting customers that are younger increases the chance of getting a purchase. The final model could predict if a customer is more likely to generate a purchase based on their age. This can also be interpreted as how much a certain customer's age will increase or decrease the chance of making a purchase from a campaign.

Just like other models in the linear regression family, logistic models are easy to interpret. However, they require users to be familiar with odds and probability. In our example of a marketing campaign, the model can tell you if there is a probability that specific characteristics in a customer is likely to lead to a sale or subscription. This type of model is also easy to update with new data and to make predictions of future observations (if there is a risk that a customer will no longer use your company's service, for example). However, just like the other regression types, the simplicity of logistic regression can cause problems when dealing with complex problems.

Now that we understand a few basic ways to interpret data and show relationships between individual variables, let's move on to something a little more complex that can be applied easily in online marketing.

Classification

Classification algorithms, also known as classifiers, are used to put observations into defined groups. For example, it is known that some customers respond well to marketing emails, and some do not. Wouldn't it be great to know which customers will respond *before* sending the emails so you can target the right people with the best personalization? This is a typical problem that can be solved with a classification algorithm. The algorithms explained in this section all handle multi-class problems, meaning they can classify data into more than two groups. For example, they can be used to classify customers as low spenders, medium spenders, or high spenders, and then to study what characteristics affect how much they spend.

In this section, we will cover four different algorithms that can be used for the classification of data. They are appropriate when seeking information about what kind of customers are most likely to respond on an offer, or to examine what strategy works best for a specific market. We'll begin with one of the simplest to understand and move on to more complex models as we go.

Decision Trees

A decision tree is a way of classifying information by sorting data based on attributes. We can think of this sorting like a set of decisions a person makes. For example, let's say you want to purchase a new car. The dealer can help find you the right model by asking a series of questions. Are you single or married? Do you have kids? What is your age and salary? Do you drive mostly in the city or in the country? With each question, the dealer helps to classify you into a certain group. If you are single with a high salary living in a city, the dealer might suggest a sporty convertible, but if you have kids and a moderate salary, they might suggest a more affordable minivan.

This type of progression can be expressed in data science as well. An algorithm can create interpretable rules similar to if/then/else statements by examining the structure of data. In our example, *if* you are single, *then* you need less space in the car. *If* you have a high salary, *then* you might want to buy a flashier vehicle.

Another example is a bank considering a loan to a client. *If* the client has the right credit score, *then* the bank will offer a loan; otherwise (*else*), the loan will not be approved. By creating a complex decision tree with many layered variables about the client (income, payment history, assets, etc.), the model can be used to predict if they are likely to repay their loan, and with what conditions.

Decision trees divide data into a number of nodes where every decision rule is a branch. At the beginning, all the data are gathered in the root node. The algorithm then scans the data's attributes to find the one that would give the best partition.

Let's consider a simplified example of a business problem using the figure below. The tree is trying to sort customers into the groups 'responding to newsletters' (Yes) vs. 'not responding' (No). The branch to the right leads directly to an output with the rule: Has the customer purchased an item in the last week? Yes. This means that the customer is directly classified as 'responding to newsletters.' On the left branch, we see that the customer did not purchase an item in the last week. It then branches again to give us more information about these people by dividing them into new and existing customers. The decision tree in the figure would tell us to send the newsletter to two types of customers: those who have purchased an item in the last week and those who haven't purchased an item last week and are new customers.

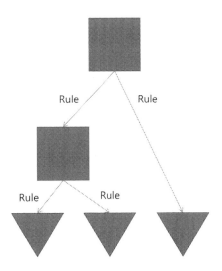

This type of algorithm chooses the attribute that generates the cleanest nodes when divided, meaning those with the clearest divisions of data (repayment vs non-repayment, or responders vs non-responders). When there are no more useful branches, meaning the attributes of a group of people are not dividing data any further, the data has reached a leaf node. This represents a classification of a specific type of person, separated by their attributes from the other leaf nodes.

When constructing a decision tree, the aim is to classify and predict the outcome with as few decisions (branches) as possible to reduce complexity and avoid overfitting. This makes the algorithm effective and efficient when just a few input variables contribute the majority of the required information.

Because it is important to use as few branches as possible, it is crucial to choose the right variable to divide on, meaning which aspect of the group will divide the data the most. Let's say that we have a hundred people, where fifty of them are customers who respond to emails and fifty do not. We then want to find which variable separates responders and non-responders the most cleanly into different nodes. Are responders more likely to be elderly? Are non-responders likely to live in the country with lower internet speeds? The attribute that helps us divide the data cleanly will help us understand our customers, and why some people respond to outreach while others do not.

Different measurements can be used in an algorithm to determine what variable to use to divide the data and when examining a tree, the goal is to determine how important certain branches are and how many branches are needed to explain the data.

Decision trees do not need too much training data to become accurate, and it does not take long to collect the necessary data. Decision trees can handle both categorical (like age groups or gender) and continuous variables (which can take on any value, like the horsepower of a car). They can also work well with outliers, which simplifies the process and thus decreases time and money spent in the modeling phase.

The way decision trees classify data is easy to understand. Now, let's look at another approach that uses a different set of rules to group information.

K-Nearest Neighbor

K-nearest neighbor (K-NN) is another classification algorithm that is easy to understand and work with. Because it is simple, it is a good way to grasp the basics of machine learning and become familiar with the fundamentals of data handling and algorithm implementation. Like the other examples we've seen, this algorithm also comes with some downsides, and K-NN is not recommended for large data sets and complex problems.

Even so, it can be appropriate for detecting outliers in data (called anomaly detection), to recommend content for system users (recommendation systems), and for search engines when trying to understand an intended search (semantic searching).

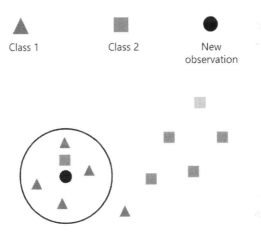

K-nearest neighbor works by detecting and analyzing the nearest observations to the new data that you wish to classify. The K is simply the number of observations that the data scientist has chosen for the algorithm. For example, let's say you're at an outdoor concert. If a data scientist wants to predict which country you are from, the K-NN could be used to help narrow that down. Let's say we set the K value to five. This means the system (or data scientist) will check the five people nearest to you to determine their country of origin. Let's say that four of the people closest to you are from Sweden and one is from Norway. From this knowledge, the algorithm would assume that you are from Sweden because most of the people around you are too. Consider this example in the figure above where you are the black dot. Since K is set to five, we will check the five nearest observations (the square and triangular shapes in the circle). Since the majority of the five observations are triangles (from Sweden) and only one is a square (from Norway) you will be classified as a triangle (Swedish).

K-nearest neighbor is a simple algorithm that is easy to set up. It is also flexible because the number of K neighbors and the distance between them are chosen for what is appropriate for the data being analyzed. However, it can be difficult to figure out which variables (attributes) to use for classification. If irrelevant variables are added, the calculated distance can be misleading and the model will perform poorly. This error can be reduced by weighting the variables (in other words, giving some more value than others in the model) by deciding which aspects of the issue are more important. K-NN also requires lots of computer memory space because the algorithm needs all the historical data points to predict a new observation. Rather than summarizing the data into a simple model, it compares older observations and classifies the new observations into similar groups. The complexity of this means the calculations can take a long time to produce effective observations.

If decision trees are straightforward ways to sort data using if-then rules and K-NN allows for more abstract sorting using similarities, the next approach adds another level to the issue: probability.

Naïve Bayes

Unlike the other classification algorithms described, the naïve bayes classifier uses a straightforward statistical approach. It builds upon conditional probability theory, where an observation is classified by computing the likelihood of it belonging to a certain group. Let's say we want to know what type of platform a certain customer is most willing to use to find information about your company. They may use their computer to look online, use the browser on their smartphone to read the mobile site, or load your company's own app. Based on the attributes of the observed customer, for example a female between 20-30 years old with a college education, the naïve bayes approach will compute the probability of that customer using a phone application, computer website, or a mobile website and classify her into the class with the highest probability. Naïve bayes is one of the tools used to do this, and it can be a helpful addition to our toolbox.

Although the algorithm is called naïve, it is a faster way to classify information about customers based on probability, rather than relying on huge data sets. This helps reduce to load on the AI system and keeps the output manageable and effective.

Since naïve bayes classifiers do not need a model to be trained, they are easy and quick to implement. This allows for testing on real data without spending a lot of time and money on developing the model. When implemented, they are quick to make predictions. The naïve bayes algorithm does not need much data to perform well and can be used on both binary and multiple class predictions, which further reduces the time and money spent on modeling. However, as the name indicates, the classifier is naïve. It requires assumptions that do not always hold up, which may cause the system to perform poorly.

For our final classifier, we'll look at neural networks. These are complex because data moves through them in elaborate ways, rather than the relatively simple systems we've seen so far.

Neural Networks

Artificial neural networks (ANN) are the most complex of the algorithms we will cover here, and our explanation has been simplified to avoid getting lost in the weeds of the issue. Simply put, they are inspired by the way human brains process information through a large number of interconnected neurons. Even though artificial neural networks can't measure up with real brains, the method has proven effective for solving difficult problems like voice recognition, image recognition, and learning to recognize handwriting.

Each neuron, also known as a node, receives input from one or multiple nodes within the network, or from an external source. Each input has its own individual weight, or importance. When receiving some input, the node applies a non-linear function, called an activation function, to the sums of its weighted input and produces an output. In simpler terms, all nodes perform a computation on the information they receive.

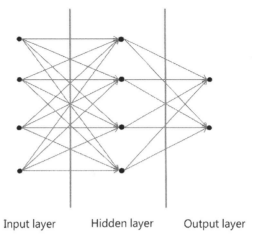

Input layer   Hidden layer   Output layer

Nodes are divided into three different layers, as shown in the image above. The first layer, called the input layer, receives input (data) from an external source. The outputs from the nodes in the input layer are then weighted and passed on to the second layer, called the hidden layer, where intermediate computation is performed. This step is complex, but for our purposes just know that the computation being done in the hidden layer uses weighted outputs from several nodes—that is, information from several places in the network. There can be a number of hidden layers and the complexity increases with the number of hidden layers. When a neural network contains more than one hidden layer it is referred to as deep learning. The output from the nodes in the hidden layer(s) are also weighted and passed on to the output layer, where the result is computed. By performing all these computations in different steps, the algorithm can find hidden patterns in the data. There are several computations in different steps, in which the output from one computation is "merged" with the output from other computations, and these are computed together to get a new output. In other words, information doesn't go through a neural network in a straightforward way, as we saw with other systems. Here, the information is used for calculations at several points, and the results then feed back into the system for further analysis.

With this complex structure, neural networks can almost simulate how a brain process information, though not nearly at the same scale. After training the network, the nodes then learn to react to different inputs. For example, if we input the information that a customer has been loyal to your company for ten years and lives in a big city, the nodes in the input will react to this information and send the reaction forward to the hidden layer. This will trigger a reaction (computation) in the hidden layer. The reactions in the hidden layer are then gathered in the output layer, which also creates a reaction. In this case, it may be that the customer is likely to use the online shop.

Artificial neural networks are complex and hard to grasp at first sight, and we can only scratch the surface of them here. Using this type of algorithm demands a lot of trust in data and in the data scientist. The issue is that as a business executive, you cannot count on understanding the conditions for a certain outcome. However, this is also the advantage of using an artificial neural network: they can handle relationships that are more complex than what can be explained without them.

Artificial neural networks have a complex structure that gives them the ability to detect hidden patterns and non-linear relationships, and to work well with classification. Due to their complex structure, artificial neural networks can find relationships that would be hard, or even impossible, to assume from the beginning and therefore could be missed when using a simpler algorithm.

Although neural networks may work well for some problems, they are not suitable for all. Sometimes a task requires interpretation and explanation, and since these types of networks are based on many connections and computations, it is hard to explain what the results are based on. Even if the task does not require explanation, it can cast doubt on the output of the model when its function is too complex to understand. Data scientists can test the result by comparing predictions with observed outputs, but this isn't always enough to justify the model's downsides.

Another issue is that it takes time to train a model, and as the number of hidden layers increases, the model becomes increasingly complex. This creates the risk of overfitting and increases the required investment in time and money.

Clearly, neural networks are an enormous topic onto themselves that fills whole books. Here, we've looked at some of the key attributes of these systems to help show how they differ from other forms of classification. Next, we'll look at a concept called clustering, which is another way to group and analyze data used by AI systems.

Clustering

As seen in the previous section, we can classify data into defined groups in a number of ways. However, what if we don't know a lot about our data? This is where clustering algorithms step in. A cluster is simply a group of observations that are close together based on some similarity, be it physical distance or another measure. For example, in a restaurant, each table could be said to be clusters of guests.

These algorithms are used to put observations into groups that we did not know existed. For example, if we are trying to get to know our customers that visit our company's website, a clustering algorithm could be used to group them and allow us to examine the different groups. We can then understand which customers are alike, how they differ, and what their characteristics are.

In this section, we will become familiar with three algorithms that approach clustering problems in different ways. Each is useful when analyzing how pieces of data are related and to help understand those relationships. We'll begin with the simplest of these algorithms, called K-means. Like the K-nearest neighbor approach described above, this one uses groups and distances to understand complex sets of data, but this time, it doesn't know what it is looking for.

K-Means

K-means is an algorithm that segments data into clusters to study similarities. This includes information on customer behavior, which can be used for targeted marketing.

The system looks at similarities between observations (for example, customers) and establishes a centroid, which is the center of a cluster. The algorithm then determines the similarities between for example customers by assigning clusters belonging to each observation to the nearest centroid. An appropriate measurement (defined by the data scientist) is used to determine the distance between observations and centroids. Don't worry if that doesn't make sense—we'll get there.

Let's go back to the outdoor concert mentioned earlier. This time, instead of trying to determine a previously known group like we did when classifying a person's country of origin, we want to know if there actually are groups of similar people in the audience. When we begin, we don't know what clusters exist, meaning we don't know what characteristics to use to group people in the crowd. However, perhaps we find that close to the stage there is a group of people (cluster 1), by the side is another group (cluster 2), and in the middle is a third group (cluster 3). Once we recognize that these clusters exist, we can then find out what variable keeps them together. Perhaps cluster 1 is a group of friends, cluster 2 is a school class, and cluster 3 is a mix of people who bought their tickets at the same time and ended up standing together.

To train a model, the algorithm first needs to know how many clusters to segment the data into. Choosing the right number of clusters can be tricky and requires exploration and testing. When the number of clusters is set, K-means starts with randomly assign initial centroids. Remember that we began by not knowing where the clusters are. To start, we randomly set one centroid (the arbitrary center of a cluster) to be in the back, one in the front, and one on the right side of the concert. From this, the K-means algorithm looks around the centroids to find the points nearby. It then updates where the centroids are located to try to find the middle of the groups that seem to exist. In the example of our second cluster, the school class, the centroid would try to find the middle of that group of people. Eventually, it finds the place in the crowd that is closest to all members of that cluster without taking in other people in the crowd. After all the adjustments are made, the algorithm sees that there can be no more refinement and stops moving.

This is quite useful in marketing because it allows us to segment large groups of customers and study them based on their behavior or other shared attributes. It discovers commonalities that may not have been apparent before, allowing for more effective targeting and outreach.

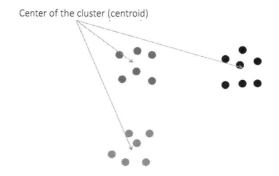

Center of the cluster (centroid)

As with all approaches, there are advantages and disadvantages here. On one hand, K-means is easy to implement, meaning it can be experimented with and analyzed without a huge cost or investment of time. It has also been proven quite effective despite the risk that poorly chosen centroids can lead the model to become stuck in false clusters, meaning it thinks it's found a cluster that is really two different clusters, for example. It is also useful because the algorithm can handle a huge amount of data. As we discussed earlier, the more data that can be used, the clearer and more accurate the results will be. Using an algorithm that can handle that scale is important.

On the other hand, there are problems with K-means that can make it less useful in some cases. For example, it performs poorly when clusters of data are not round (when data points are scattered, for example if our school class doesn't stand together in a circle at the concert), or when clusters have different densities, meaning when observations in some clusters are farther apart. It can also be difficult to determine how many clusters of data to use to create your desired result.

Issues with the shape and distribution of clusters can be remedied in some cases by using the next in our list of clustering algorithms, called DBSCAN.

DBSCAN

The density-based spatial clustering of applications with noise algorithm (DBSCAN) uses clustering by finding groups of observations with a high density, meaning they are not spread out. This is appropriate if the clusters can be assumed to have different shapes. This differs from k-means because it can accommodate different shapes in data instead of only round clusters. This allows an analysis to pull other observations from the data and help to find similarities that can otherwise go unnoticed.

DBSCAN requires two parameters. The first is called epsilon, which looks at the maximum distance away a data point can be to still be part of the group. The other parameter is MinPoints, which dictates the minimum number of similar observations in a group required to be included in that cluster. So, if you set MinPoint to five, then even if an observation has a distance less than the epsilon to three observations, it would still be excluded from the cluster. As you might notice, DBSCAN doesn't require that we tell the algorithm how many clusters to find. Not having to select the number of clusters simplifies the task of getting new information out from data and reduces the risk of missing out of important or hidden knowledge.

This sounds complicated, but these types of clustering algorithms have a unique function in marketing. For instance, they can used to recommend products to a cluster of customers based on what they have previously purchased. If one customer in a cluster has purchased product A and product B, and another customer in the same cluster has purchased product A as well, then we could recommend product B for the second customer. Amazon's site does something similar when it recommends purchases based on what other people bought.

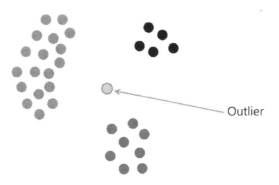

Outlier

As you can tell, clustering can be a complex issue, but also quite helpful in understanding and working with data. In the final example, we'll look at agglomerative hierarchical clustering. Let's jump in, but don't let the name scare you!

Agglomerative Hierarchical Clustering

Sometimes when looking at a set of data, the number of clusters isn't distinct. This is where agglomerative hierarchical clustering is useful. Imagine that you just launched a new product and you don't know how the customers are using it. You want to study this, but because it is a new product, you don't have much knowledge on customer behavior.

Instead of being told how many clusters there should be, hierarchical clustering seeks the appropriate number of clusters first. By starting with a collection of unclustered data or observations, the points are then merged one by one until all observations are in the same cluster. This is done by taking the nearest clusters in each step and grouping them together. For example, imagine a hundred people spread out on a football field. At the beginning, they each stand by themselves, essentially meaning there are a hundred clusters (each with one person). The two people closest to each other are then asked to move together, which reduces the number of clusters to ninety-nine (one cluster has two people). Eventually, if you repeat this instruction enough times, there will be single cluster with a hundred people. The same approach is used for customers when studying purchasing habits.

Each merging is then studied to determine the right number of clusters for the issue at hand. This is done by examining how far away the clusters were when they merged. On the football field, the first people clustered together were close already, but after a few more times merging with groups, the distance between the different clusters will grow. You may have a large cluster at one end of the field, and another at the far end. This system lets the data scientist decide how many clusters to use after establishing how far is too far for clusters to merge with each other. In marketing terms, this means it creates groups of different types of customers, but focuses on deciding how similar they have to be to target in the same way. For example, you might target an ad for a barbeque at young families living in rural areas and older couples in a suburb because they share the attribute of having outdoor space for cooking. However, you would not target the ad to young families or older couples living in an apartment building.

Agglomerative hierarchical clustering does not require initial centroids or prior knowledge of the number of clusters, which reduces the amount of analysis required on the data before using this approach.

Although we won't get into them all here, there are different techniques to choose from, depending on what is appropriate for the data set. This makes it more flexible and provides an opportunity to explore and find the appropriate algorithm. On the downside, the algorithm cannot handle large data sets, which makes it less useful for some tasks.

Chapter Summary

Choosing an appropriate algorithm is crucial for several reasons, including its effectiveness in your project, how much time and money you are willing to spend, your level of expertise, and what has been done already in the project. Some algorithms are too specialized to solve a certain type of problem, while others overlap and can be used in multiple ways.

Regardless what kind of marketing problem you may come across, there will usually be an algorithm suitable to help you understand or solve the issue—or at least give you an indication of what to do next.

This chapter has provided an introduction to some of the most widely used algorithms. They can be simple or complex, and each handles a specific type of problem. If you take one thing from this chapter, I hope that it is that algorithms and models should be as simple as possible to fit their purpose. As Albert Einstein said, "Keep it as simple as possible, but no simpler." Now that we understand how these algorithms differ and what they can be used for, let's put them to work.

PUTTING YOUR
AI TO WORK

Even the best prediction models are useless for any practical purposes until they are deployed to solve real life problems. Moving from the data scientist's lab to the real world is crucial to the final testing and production use of the algorithms. Let's look at the process of implementing these solutions to make them most useful for your company.

Making Predictions

To be practically useful, the prediction models must be implemented as software and run on a computer somewhere. Secondly, some business application (like a cloud application or smartphone app) must connect to the prediction system to get insights from new data. For a long time, it was a manual task to implement the selected algorithm into software code. Often, that meant the prediction model had to be crafted in programming languages like C#, Python, or Java.

Now, however, easy-to-use cloud services have emerged, dramatically simplifying the efforts required for development, testing, and deployment of machine learning algorithms. Examples of hosted cloud-solutions for machine learning and predictive analytics are Amazon Web Services, Google Tensorflow, and Microsoft Azure ML. Such cloud-based systems enable the development, testing, and deployment of advanced machine learning solutions with little more than a web browser and a credit card. Once developed in a programming language like R or Python, the selected prediction models can be implemented and deployed on their cloud servers with just a couple of clicks.

Your application software (like Windows programs, cloud applications, or smartphone apps) can easily access the predictions offered by those models using simple web services that can be consumed from applications written in almost any other programming language. This type of cloud-based machine learning platform democratizes the development of AI, as it is now available at relatively low cost and skill threshold, provided you know how to develop the algorithm itself. Microsoft .NET now includes machine learning modules too.

Effectively, the barrier to entry for developing your own machine learning solutions is dramatically reduced, enabling a massive adoption of self-learning systems that will disrupt many industries. These ready-made machine learning platforms will likely drive AI penetration to a scale never seen before.

Changing Conditions Require Retraining

So far, we have covered an overview of different types of AI algorithms, and how prediction models are developed and put in production use. Let's take a step back and see how the retraining of predictive analytics systems turns them into machine learning systems in some more detail. This is key to understanding AI, so it's worth exploring in more detail. As we move forward, we'll add complexity to these systems to build a better understanding of how today's algorithms work in the real world.

Predictive analytics systems are designed to detect a particular pattern, but if that pattern changes over time, the model will not adapt unless it is retrained from new data. Effectively, an untouched prediction model will become increasingly imprecise if environment conditions change.

For example, take product recommendations in a web shop. As autumn starts, fewer and fewer customers will buy swim gear, and more people will purchase autumn or winter clothes instead. A product recommendation engine must adapt to such changes to remain useful. As outlined above, prediction models draw heavily from historical data, and in that sense, they can be said to be trained by data. However, this is because a data scientist performed iterative experiments until a winning model candidate was found, and it was largely a one-off event handled manually.

If the data patterns change over time, like seasonality in a sports shop, the prediction model will not adjust to this change. Thus, the model must be re-trained to refresh its behavior such that it continues to make accurate predictions when the environment changes. Several factors go into this, and the retraining frequency depends on how quickly the data patterns being predicted change.

When the model is retrained, the updated model must be deployed for production use, and therefore replace the older model. If done manually, this retraining is likely not implemented frequently, and it takes time and effort each time it's undertaken. This is where continuous retraining comes in.

Continuous Retraining

Self-training is implemented by adding a feedback loop in which the model adjusts itself as new data become available over time. This is what turns a prediction model into a machine learning system. It is required to build a system that can adapt to changes in its environment, for example, what products to recommend depending on the time of year or weather conditions.

Manual re-training might not be the best solution, as time and effort must be scheduled to import and process new training data into the model all the time. Clearly, we would benefit from a self-learning model that can re-train itself automatically as new data becomes available. This is exactly what machine learning platforms can do; they record any new data that becomes available and re-train and re-deploy themselves continuously. In effect, they learn continuously and adapt their behavior automatically from additional data.

This was science fiction to most people not so long ago, but it is more or less a commodity today. Now, any marginally skilled software developer can create systems using advanced self-learning prediction systems with continuous retraining.

Hardware Accelerated and Distributed AI

We've spent some time discussing machine learning solutions that are completely implemented in software—that is, deployed in large computer systems like cloud servers. This is the predominant model, particularly for processing marketing data. However, new developments are coming with the introduction of special electronic chips that implement machine learning technology into silicon. In other words, these algorithms are being implemented into the core of the hardware itself. While this isn't likely to affect your business directly any time soon, it's an indication of where this technology is headed. As AI-powered hardware develops, we will begin to see even smarter devices and the use of AI in unexpected places.

With machine learning systems implemented into electronic hardware rather than software, we can improve prediction performance by magnitudes using small electronic circuits that fit inside small devices like smartphones or cameras. Just like microprocessor devices made many products 'smart' a decade or two ago, the same products may now become equipped with machine learning chips. We are entering a world of distributed AI, where advanced machine learning solutions aren't exclusively used in centralized servers, but are integrated into small everyday objects as well.

nVIDIA, for example, is using their expertise in graphics cards for PCs to sell high-performing machine learning hardware, with autonomous self-driving cars being the most obvious target market. In effect, they offer machine-learning supercomputers the size of an ordinary lunch box intended to be the brain of autonomous cars and similar products. Retail marketing might be another use for this type of highly powerful machine-learning hardware. It can, for example, drive real-time responses from image analysis of multiple live HD video streams. Perhaps they can be used to analyze the sentiment, age, gender, clothing style (and thus financial status), and behavior of store visitors as well. Such insights could be gathered from live HD video streams to personalize the message of in-store digital signage, email marketing, and more. That would turn the personalized billboards in Stephen Spielberg's *The Minority Report* into a reality. It seems futuristic, but it's closer than you think.

A related technology based on distributed neural networks is being developed by AiFi, located more or less across the street from nVIDIA's headquarter in Santa Clara. They are developing a solution for retail stores that uses image analysis from multiple live video streams to create checkout-free stores. A network of downward-looking cameras is installed in the ceiling, tracking how shoppers move and behave. The cameras detect who is taking what products from the shelves automatically, thus adding the cost to the bill. If you put the product back on the shelf, the price is deducted again. Effectively, AI-powered vision systems that replace the cashiers enable "grab and go" retail stores.

With such solutions, the cashiers aren't needed, and shoplifting is something of the past; you can't steal anything, as grabbing something from the shelf means you are charged for it. Customers get increased convenience, and the stores get more information on how their customers behave, reduced staff cost, and real-time inventory management. In fact, stores like this already exist. Amazon Go is a grocery store that allows customers to scan a card when they enter, shop for whatever they want, and leave without interacting with the checkout at all. Their credit card or bank account is charged automatically, and they get a receipt on their smartphone when they leave the shop.

Apple was one of the first companies to ship machine learning hardware at a massive scale with the introduction of the iPhone X, which contains a neural engine that provides hardware accelerated machine learning. The company also offers a software development kit, enabling iOS app developers to easily integrate machine learning into their iPhone and iPad apps. With Core ML, app developers can integrate computer vision (face tracking, object detection, etc.) and natural language processing for text understanding into their apps.

Arm, the semiconductor IP company (whose microprocessor designs are used in virtually every smartphone and tablet on the market, and in most Internet-of-Things devices as well), has announced a plan to launch designs for machine learning chips as well. That move will enable tens of thousands of manufacturers of ordinary products with integrated electronics to add machine learning capabilities onto the electronic boards that drive the logic of those products. Think microwave ovens, burglar alarms, industrial sensors, consumer electronics, and more here. They might all become equipped with their own machine learning chip to make them even smarter. Although it might be difficult to envision a microwave with AI capabilities today, if the adoption of smart phones and tablets is any indication, soon they will be ubiquitous and tasked with solving problems we didn't even know we had.

We might soon go from a world there AI is predominantly handled by business software in cloud servers to one with distributed AI built around neural network chips added to everyday objects. We can only imagine how that will change the dynamics of many markets. What additional insights will that give marketers? We won't have to wait long to find out.

Chapter Summary

In this chapter, we looked at how prediction algorithms are implemented as prediction models, which are then deployed as web services that other types of software can consume. We learned that the difference between a prediction system and a machine learning system is a feedback loop where new data automatically and continuously re-trains the model. Finally, we saw that new advances in machine learning electronics may disrupt the current model where AI solutions are predominantly implemented as cloud server services, potentially offering new opportunities to the field of marketing. Next, we'll look at how all of these changes might affect your business, and what you can do about it.

HOW WILL AI AFFECT MY BUSINESS?

While this book covers how to perform data-driven marketing with AI, we need to give some thought to related fields as well. With AI disrupting industries and companies around the world, many people are asking:

- Will AI replace my marketing job?
- Will AI disrupt my company or industry?

These are important questions and their answers will have widespread impacts in the years to come. Let's spend some time looking at these issues in more detail.

Will AI Replace My Marketing Job?

With artificial intelligence able to handle so many marketing tasks, one might wonder if AI-bots will augment marketers, or simply make their jobs obsolete entirely. I've discussed this with many AI experts, and the consensus seems to be that AI-bots absolutely will replace many marketing tasks, particularly those that have to do with analysis, decision making based on numerical data, and repetitive tasks.

The benefit here is that this leaves more time for working on strategy and the creative side of things. AI systems should primarily be seen as tools that analyze vast amounts of data automatically, reduce tedious repetitive work, and improve the output of our working days—much like machinery has already done in manufacturing. There's nothing new here really, except that now it is happening to highly skilled and well-paid professionals. Like in the restructuring of other industries in the past, the repetitive and routine tasks will be removed first. If you plan and analyze ad spending, harvest market and competitor intelligence from public websites, or try to surface insights from internal databases, your job may soon be replaced, since these tasks are done more quickly and efficiently by AI.

Content creators, for example copywriters of blog posts or website copy, are probably in the middle of the spectrum, you will likely use AI tools to understand what topics and keywords to cover, and how to write for best SEO juice or reader engagement. But the actual writing will probably be done manually, at least for a few more years. If you design graphic creatives, you are probably safe a few more years too, but you will get AI-assisted graphic design tools, for example to determine what design permutations drive the best ad ROI.

If your work is fully strategic, or mostly related to managing people or meeting customers, you don't need to worry too much for a while. However, it is likely that your work will be a lot more data-driven, and there may be changes to the staff or their work-tasks in your team.

Generally, the more your job relates to repetitive work or work that has to do with analyzing data one way or another, you may want to consider picking up some new skills and education to ensure a safer future. On the other hand, the more strategic or creative your work is, you will likely keep your job, though it will change in nature. AI will, for the most part, augment and automate marketing jobs, rather than replacing most of them.

I asked industry leaders from several prominent companies if they thought marketers will be replaced by robots. Here are some of their responses:

Or Shani, CEO and founder of Albert Technologies, Inc:

"No. The key here is to understand that AI takes on the time-consuming data management/analysis work in order to free the marketer to focus on higher-level strategic and creative work. The marketer remains in control and the AI makes decisions, within "guardrails" or guidelines established by the marketer. It follows logic that machines continue to do what they do best so that humans can focus on human creative efforts instead of wading through massive amounts of data, a task which humans are not built to complete as efficiently as machines or AI.

Further to this, the conversation should be a focus on the relationship between man and machine and leveraging one another's strengths to optimize the initiative. AI technology is supplemental to the success of any digital marketing campaign and the sooner marketer's understand this the sooner they can prepare their organization and staff for AI adoption."

Mike Mallazzo, Head of content at Dynamic Yield:

"No. While automation presents a very credible threat to many industries, AI is actually poorly suited to replace marketers. Despite the predictions of futurists, AI has yet to show a propensity to accomplish any creative tasks. At the end of the day, while companies may turn some logistical jobs to AI, we are decades away from AI building brands.

Ultimately, AI will make marketers jobs better in the same way that it will improve quality of professional life for most knowledge workers. AI will eliminate hours of tedium and allow marketers to spend less time on mundane tasks and more time on more fulfilling work that requires truly human intellect."

Brennan White, CEO and Co-founder of Cortex

"Specific marketing jobs are already being replaced by AI. But marketing as a profession will only become more valuable as the ROI of marketing increases. Marketing jobs will become more numerous as the executives see a clearer and more significant ROI on marketing.

Google is actually the best example of what happens when a business becomes massively profitable. Google's core business (advertising) is so successful that it's able to fund thousands of employees and many other entire business units. As AI infuses into marketing and companies see a clearer and larger profit from dollars invested in that business unit, they will invest in marketing more heavily."

Jeremy Miller, Vice President of Marketing at Sentient Technologies

"AI will allow marketers to be more efficient but not necessarily replace them. As marketing becomes more and more data centric, AI will help alleviate some of the heavy lifting and complexity of managing disparate campaigns. It will allow marketers to get back to doing what they do best, coming up with strategic ideas and creative campaigns instead of asking them to turn into data scientists."

These are valuable insights, and it's likely reassuring to note that even experts in the field believe marketing jobs will be safe in the years to come. However, it's safe to assume that not all positions will remain, or will stay the same as they are now. For that, let's look at some ways to add to your qualifications to make you more competitive as AI becomes more dominant in the years to come.

How to Position Yourself

Even in disruptive times, there are always opportunities to leverage. How should you position yourself to make the most out of this technological shift? One approach is to become the AI evangelist in your company. Foster a mindset of exploration and learning, and be ready to try out new tools and techniques. The fact you are reading this book indicates you are already on this path, and you should be fine!

Further, educating yourself on marketing technology (martech), including marketing automation and artificial intelligence, can't hurt. Most marketing jobs will be increasingly data-driven, and hence software based. Try to learn the software solutions used in data-driven marketing and stay ahead of the curve on new developments. You don't need to become a data scientist to remain a marketer, but raising your skills in marketing technology—such as marketing automation software—will help you stay relevant and competitive.

Lean away from job roles that most involve repetitive or routine tasks, in particular those that relate to analyzing data. If your job is to gather insights from data in one way or the other, I would try to step up the value chain and learn more about the tools that eventually will replace such manual work. Instead of analyzing competitor activities, for example, learn as much as you can about the tools that automate such tasks, or the strategies used to combat competitors. Instead of passively watching your job being replaced, become the evangelist that is forward-looking enough to introduce the tools to your company.

I spend a large part of my working life staying on top of these issues. My blog is a good place to learn more about how AI is changing the world of marketing and what you can do to stay ahead: *www.unemyr.com/blog*

I also recommend these two blogs for insightful and up to date information on the field: *http://chiefmartec.com* and *http://marketingaiinstitute.com*

Should you be interested in more thorough AI training, there are many courses available through Google, Coursera, and on YouTube.

Will AI Disrupt My Company or Industry?

Beyond worrying about our own jobs, it's worth looking at how our business or industry will cope. In some industries, the situation might be a bit alarming. I suspect we will see a big shift in the business models of many industries in the future. For example, the sharing economy and subscription models will likely continue to grow. Combined with autonomous and self-optimizing systems, this will drive a significant shift in how society works, disrupting entire industries, or at least portions of value chains.

Although this isn't strictly part of using AI in marketing, it is important for business leaders and marketers to be aware of how AI can affect them in other ways too. If you aren't prepared for how AI might affect your company, then it won't matter how you execute your marketing plan. Take self-driving cars as an example.

Most cars have a high purchase price and are only used for driving for a short time each day, and some days they aren't used at all. Until recently, owning your own car has been the only convenient model, but with AI enabling self-driving cars, this model will be disrupted. If the car can drive itself, there is no need to own your own vehicle anymore. It would only be parked in your garage unused most of the time anyway, representing a tremendously poor utilization of the investment, and locking up space you could use for something else.

Once cars are fully self-driving, you could simply click a button on your smartphone, and one will arrive from your city's car sharing service. You could schedule one in advance, or even have a recurring travel schedule. With predictive analytics, car sharing companies can predict where the cars need to be in advance, thus shortening wait times. RethinkX's industry report on transportation suggests that 95% of all passenger miles in the USA will be served by fleets of self-driving cars by 2030, using a "transport-as-a-service" (TaaS) business model. [15] This will have incredible implications.

The cost of transportation may be reduced by 90%, since the financial investment can be shared over many users and the utilization of cars becomes massively increased. AI-based routing optimization will further improve utilization and thus improve the cost efficiency. This will all drive down the average cost per transportation mile, perhaps by an order of magnitude.

With such a low cost of transportation in metropolitan areas, you might even get the transport for free if you accept watching ads, or if you purchase some goods while in the vehicle. Starbucks on wheels comes to mind. If passengers buy a cup of coffee and a muffin, the ride might otherwise be free. RethinkX believes the average American family will save over $5,600 per year, which is equivalent to a wage increase of 10%, totaling $1 trillion yearly that American families can spend on other things.

Furthermore, car sharing might reduce the need for new cars by 70% or more. This will obviously be disruptive to car manufacturers, and their first-, second-, and third-tier suppliers. There will be no demand for the majority of their current production volumes. This will create a domino effect all the way down to steelworks and mines, which will see a dramatic reduction in demand from the auto industry. Companies supplying machinery or other services to all tiers of the supply chain will suffer equally. Convenient car sharing services, enabled by self-driving cars, will affect jobs in many other industries too. There will be no need for driving schools or highway patrol, for example. This is to say nothing of taxi drivers, bus drivers, delivery van drivers, and truck drivers who will be made redundant. Add waste collectors and farmers driving tractors on

15   "Rethinking Transportation," RethinkX, 2017. *https://www.rethinkx.com/transportation*

fields, and many more. There will be almost no need for staff handling personal car insurance or bank loans for car purchases.

Given this, one might suspect the automotive industry and dependent industries are in for a shock of historical proportions. However, it doesn't stop there. If your company serves the car industry, it can get worse. The reason is electric cars. Once the majority of cars are electrified, many parking lots will double as recharging stations. Thus, there will be no need for petrol stations anymore, and their staff and supply chain will be out of jobs. The need for oil will be dramatically reduced, creating a price collapse in the industry. All dependent industries will be affected as well, including chemical laboratories, off-shore technology suppliers, and shipyards. Many companies will be completely wiped out by this change.

On the positive side, parking lots in city centers will become redundant. Self-driving cars will drop you off and continue on to their next task. Thus, cities may reclaim all the space used for parking. This will change how space is used in cities, allowing more trees to be planted along streets that were previously filled with parked cars. Cafes and green areas can take their place, improving the quality of life for residents.

Electric cars are designed differently than traditional cars with combustion engines, and as we will soon see, this will put more pressure on some industries that depend on cars. Electric cars have far fewer moving parts, meaning they need less maintenance, fewer spare parts, and fewer hours in the garage. Many auto shops will not survive.

Finally, self-driving buses will create a dramatic shift in how public transport works. Currently, the driver is a large portion of the cost of operating a bus. This cost must be offset by having many passengers in each bus. Hence, they don't operate in areas with few passengers, largely due to the cost of the driver. With self-driving vehicles, small buses carrying fewer passengers become economically feasible. This means the network of public transport can be much larger, reaching less densely populated areas of a city. This assumes buses will even survive the cost-effective transport-as-a-service solutions from car sharing services. More likely,

TaaS fleets and public transportation will merge into a new form of getting around.

This example is extreme and isn't directly tied to marketing, but it highlights how AI and other technological advances will disrupt many industries in the years to come. These disruptions will create a domino effect that will completely change market dynamics throughout the supply chains. Any forward-looking business leader or marketer must be aware of how such transformational changes will affect their industry. If you are wise, move fast and leverage these developments to your advantage. Adapt your product and service offerings to this new future—it will be here sooner than you think.

Chapter Summary

Throughout this book, we have seen how AI can empower marketers in many ways. In this chapter, we looked at how we as marketers, our businesses, and our industry might be affected. Much of this is speculation, of course, but with transformational changes come both risks and opportunities. In the next chapter, we will look at additional technologies beyond AI that are waiting just around the corner.

WHAT'S NEXT IN MARKETING AFTER AI?

With the current hype in predictive and AI-driven marketing, one might wonder what comes after AI. Some of what we'll discuss here might feel like science fiction, but I can assure you, this is not the case. Quite on the contrary. Let's take a journey into the (near) future.

The Internet-of-Things

I've spent most of my career marketing software that is used to develop the next generation of electronics devices. The software development tools I worked on have been used by organizations like NASA and major Japanese consumer brands, as well as some of the most well-known European and American industrial corporations. They have purchased the software to design products like drones, instruments for space missions, thermostats, automotive diagnostics, navigation systems, utility products like solar power inverters, robotics, airbags, and more.

For over two decades, I worked in what is now known as the Internet-of-Things (IoT) industry, which is an evolution of what we once called the embedded systems market. It is predicted that a trillion devices will be Internet-connected by 2025, and most of them will upload usage data to cloud servers. Currently, marketers mostly look to use AI to find predictions based on data generated by leads and customers, such as using their digital footprint or purchase history to target the right people with highly personalized marketing messages. This will soon change.

Marketing Insights from Machine-Generated Data

With a world where almost all devices are Internet-connected, machines will generate far more data than humans will. This machine-generated data can be used to find business insights that can help drive marketing.

Consider these examples:

- Bathroom scales can report weight-change patterns, enabling predictive algorithms to determine someone will likely gain weight a month down the road. Marketing automation logic can then be triggered to offer healthier food options or change the daily recipes to include fewer calories.

- Machines can detect when they are about to break down using predictive maintenance based on vibration or heat patterns. Marketing automation logic can then be triggered to offer service or send spare parts automatically to prevent the machine from breaking down in the first place.

- Training results from gym equipment can be analyzed for correlations to previous members who canceled their club memberships. Marketing outreach can then be initiated to prevent this from happening.

- The usage pattern of some device indicates the owner may be a good candidate for up-selling, cross-selling, or replenishment, and marketing automation logic can be commenced automatically to promote such options, for example using email or push notifications.

- Real-time online weather data combined with moisture sensors installed in farmers' fields can predict when more fertilizers should be ordered.

- Coffee machines or washing machines can order more coffee beans or detergent automatically based on usage patterns.

I predict that after AI-driven marketing based on data from people, the field will be driven by AI-insights based on data coming from Internet-connected machines (IoT devices). Marketing systems will react by sending email sequences, push notifications, schedule customer service tickets or sales rep phone calls, or use the data for segmentation or lead scoring. This will take autonomous marketing to the next level, far beyond what most marketers currently anticipate.

Machines Becoming Customers

Washing machines self-ordering detergent may not be as far off as you'd expect. In 2017, Amazon acquired the world's most popular real-time operating system software, which is used to develop many IoT products (the control electronics in IoT devices use real-time operating systems instead of Microsoft Windows, MacOS X, Android, or iOS).

Many people assumed this to be a move to widen the market for Amazon's data-center cloud services, which makes perfect sense from Amazon's point of view (in addition to their e-commerce business, Amazon is one of the world's largest providers of data center services for cloud hosting). If a large proportion of the trillion or so Internet-connected devices will use Amazon's operating system (which is called FreeRTOS), then it is likely that many of the companies who are developing those IoT products will look to Amazon for hosting data from those products on their cloud services as well.

After all, IoT products need to store their data in cloud servers somewhere, and if Amazon's operating system would be extended to include readymade functionality for uploading, that would be the easiest choice for developers. Thinking one step further, it is not difficult to see Amazon also extending their operating system to enable Internet-connected products to purchase products automatically from the Amazon store.

Thus, it makes perfect sense that a supplier of operating system software for IoT products also includes autonomous purchases in a web shop like Amazon. With such functionality, the potential customer base of an e-commerce site would be increased to tens or hundreds of billions of autonomous machines. This assumes the software is integrated into most of those IoT products, which might become the case with Amazon's operating system.

I expect it will not be too long before we see machines starting to make autonomous product purchases based on AI-predictions from machine-generated data. Coffee machines ordering coffee beans and washing machines ordering detergent are just a couple of examples. We might not be too far from our refrigerators ordering new milk automatically, and industrial machinery ordering new spare parts just in time. There are probably millions of examples of both B2C and B2B products that would benefit from automated purchasing.

Amazon is clearly well positioned here, as they now own the operating system that is used to develop a large share of all Internet-connected devices in the world and have the cloud services to store the data generated by those devices as well. Not to mention how the market dynamics would shift if billions of Internet-connected products were pre-programmed to order products from the Amazon web shop autonomously.

I suspect that in a world of machines making autonomous purchases, the business models will change. Rather than buying products, you will subscribe to a service that automates your repetitive purchases like milk and detergent. One can only guess how many markets will be disrupted when billions of machines start to make autonomous product purchases. This brings us to the next section, which might be a little scary to some marketers. All of this automation will change how we shop, but it also provides the perfect vendor lock-in.

How do You Market to a Machine?

If billions of machines are able to order replenishments or spare parts automatically, marketers will indeed be faced with an interesting problem never conceived before. How do you market your product to a machine that is pre-programmed to purchase a competing brand automatically?

The frightening answer for marketers is likely that you can't. Marketers will have a whole new set of problems to address in the future. Not only do you have to outperform your competition, now you need to find a way to become the pre-programmed choice in machines as well. Despite this, I have to give Amazon credit for being exceptionally visionary. Not only did they crush the e-commerce market thanks to AI-powered recommendation engines and highly efficient logistics. They also had the insight to look into a different industry entirely, that of software solutions used for development of electronic devices, to build a huge market for their data center services. That move also scales their potential customer base to include billions of machines that may start making autonomous purchases in their web shop, should they choose to enable this capability.

Hats off to you, Amazon. You made a smart move with this one. Their competitors may be cheering considerably less. It will be impossible for other firms to duplicate this move. It was an opportunity of a lifetime. The reason? Only FreeRTOS has this strong market penetration in

IoT device development, and only Amazon offers such a strong e-commerce platform combined with data center hosting services, making this practically impossible for others to replicate.

The future is certainly interesting, and traditional companies not moving fast enough will be punished. For some, it is already too late. My guess is that the big vendors will become even more dominant, and we will enter a "the winner takes all" era where the famous Pareto principle (known as the 80/20 rule) will have to give way for the just coined Unemyr principle (the 99/1 rule), where 1% of the vendors take 99% of the revenue due to the first-mover advantage in the digital markets.

Let Marketing Data Control Machines

Product development companies in control of how their Internet-connected products are designed have additional possibilities. Not only can you let data from machines drive marketing automation logic or let Internet-connected machines make autonomous product purchases on e-commerce sites. Why not use the data the other way around? We can let cloud services with marketing data control the machines you have delivered to your customers.

Let's say you offer some extra functionality in your Internet-connected physical product that can be enabled by a software upgrade. If a customer purchases this upgrade, then this functionality could be pushed out to that particular device automatically over the Internet upon receiving the order. A software protocol could update a setting on the device to enable this functionality. Alternatively, they could push a software upgrade with the new functionality automatically, using the Internet connection and remote device management protocols (see my IoT book for details on this).

If the rental period for some device is about to expire due to credit card payment problems, a text message indicating payment problems could be pushed out and be displayed on the device, or discount offers on coffee beans could be displayed on coffee machines.

Perhaps your cloud systems determine (by web service calls to the local weather service) that it is going to be dry the coming week. The lawn sprinkler system you sell will automatically be instructed to water the lawn more heavily to improve the customer experience. Maybe the marketing automation system remotely resets and restarts a device automatically when the owner files a support request using the customer service ticket system.

Another option is to let your marketing automation system control your own machines, not those of your customers. You could, for example, send a production order to your laser engraving system to start manufacturing personalized pens to those leads who have reached a certain threshold of behavior activity, or expose certain purchase patterns. The possibilities are endless and limited only by the imagination.

Blockchain

In addition to AI and IoT, another hyped technology right now is blockchain. While not powered by AI, blockchain technology has enormous potential to change the way the internet operates, and how it interacts with AI systems will be fascinating to watch in the coming years.

What is it and how can it apply to AI and marketing? Let's start with the first question. Blockchain is the foundational technology on which the crypto-currency Bitcoin is built. While there are different opinions on the merits of Bitcoin as a currency, almost everyone seems to agree blockchain is a useful technology for enabling trust in any type of transaction on the Internet. As we will soon see, it brings many benefits to online transactions.

A Trusted Ledger of Transactions

Blockchain is an incorruptible and decentralized ledger of transactions with elements of transparency, trust, and verifiability, distributed over many computers on the Internet. It is used to permanently record any transaction between two persons or entities, including monetary transactions, ownership transactions, information exchange transactions, or other types of transactions that require trust.

Each block is a cryptographic hash of the transaction data to store it securely, as well as a cryptographic hash of the previous block. Blocks of transaction data are thus chained together, hence the name blockchain. The transaction records are stored on the computers of many users across the Internet, and so with blockchain, there is no centralized server or authority. Therefore, multiple copies of a blockchain are stored in different places on the Internet, and we don't need to trust a central authority to manage the records.

You can't alter the blocks afterwards without invalidating the chain of cryptographic sealing. Furthermore, any attempt to tamper with a block can be detected, as multiple other copies of the blockchain exist across the Internet. This is because all the other copies would disagree with the change, effectively enabling consensus decision-making, or voting. The altered blockchain would be detected and identified as fraudulent.

Anyone on the blockchain can view and validate a transaction. In effect, blockchain is a technology that enables transparency, trust, and verifiability in online transactions, with unalterable historical records. Many types of transactions require some kind of broker to provide trust; for example, transferring money (banks and credit card companies), borrowing and returning books (libraries), buying or selling stocks (stock markets), or buying ad space (Google and other media exchanges).

Because transactions recorded on a blockchain are secure, the system removes the need for intermediates. This enables people or entities to make secure transaction directly, without using an intermediate broker, thus potentially changing the dynamics on those markets.

How Does Blockchain Apply to Marketing?

Ad purchasing and media brokers are examples where the intermediaries will likely be removed from the supply-chain in the future, largely due to blockchain. While Google and Facebook currently have a stranglehold in this market, there are many other media brokers as well. Blockchain may enable strong changes to this market. There are also many areas in marketing where we can leverage the improved trust that blockchain allows.

For example, blockchain might be able to verify if influencers are true influencers, meeting marketers' criteria, say, in terms of having true social media followers rather than fake followers. This can make influencer marketing a more transparent game with marketers having access to more accurate information on actual clout. Display ads are another area where blockchain might be of use. It can be hard for ad buyers to know if the ad space purchased is in fact delivered as expected—i.e. is viewed by real people rather than bots or subject to other types of fraud.

Fraud verification companies might start to use blockchain to prevent bots and fraudsters from stealing ad budgets, if they aren't already. We might be able to verify all aspects of ad views (such as who, how, where, and when) using blockchain, thus making the whole process more transparent. This reduces fraud and will improve attribution as well. Adding a layer of AI on top of blockchain might provide adaptive insights or strategy recommendations, based on more trusted data sources.

Chapter Summary

In this chapter, we looked at a few examples of other technologies that might transform marketing further, far beyond AI. I may be biased from my two decades in the software industry, but I think data from Internet-connected devices have the power to change the world. The capabilities and consequences of billions of Internet-connected devices, such as machines making autonomous product purchases, cannot be underestimated.

CHANGES TO
THE SOCIETY

It should be clear by now that advanced analytics using large amounts of data can help us gather valuable insights, but also predict the future user behavior. This will disrupt the marketing industry and help it to become more efficient and relevant again.

However, machine learning has no social awareness or ethics. It is based only on raw data and can generally not detect socially unacceptable patterns that might lead to undesirable behavior. There are legal and ethical matters to consider, and naïve use—or plain abuse—of such powerful technologies can make life hard for some. Treat the power of AI and machine learning responsibly.

Ethics

With AI comes new ethical problems. An example is the infamous story about Target's predictive marketing program that supposedly resulted in marketing for pregnant women being sent to a teenage girl. According to the story, widely spread on the Internet, Target developed a prediction algorithm that used past purchase patterns to predict when women are pregnant. The prediction algorithm allegedly sent direct marketing home to the girl, who was still living with her parents.

Supposedly, the father saw the marketing literature for pregnant women and became furious as "his teenage daughter obviously wasn't pregnant." Target had to apologize, only for the father to later learn the daughter was in fact pregnant. Later posts on the internet question the truth of this story and suggest it has been taken out of its original context, but the moral remains. Similar situations can—and will—happen with wider use of machine learning and prediction algorithms.

Marketers need to be careful with this new technology, as the effects of such automated campaigns can give unexpected and unwanted consequences for innocent people. Other problems may come from the opposite direction. For example, if the purchase pattern of someone should signal high risk of a lethal disease, say cancer, what should a grocery chain do? Should they contact health officials or alarm the subject, perhaps with a false positive? One wouldn't want to alarm customers if the prediction turned out to be incorrect, but the consequences of not raising a notification might be severe.

While such examples may seem far-fetched, they won't be for long. AI-derived insights will give us new ethical problems we haven't had to consider before. We don't have to go far to find examples.

In March 2018, a cross-Atlantic scandal erupted when it became clear that personal information on over 87 million people from Facebook could have been used by the British company Cambridge Analytica, without permission, to affect the outcome of public elections, most notably the 2016 US presidential election and the Brexit vote. That sent Facebook's CEO, Mark Zuckerberg, to Congress to testimony about privacy and the security of personal data. In the aftermath of the scandal, Cambridge Analytica shut down within weeks. The ethical risks are real.

For us marketers, having lots of data is great, as we can target our customers better, personalize messages, and be less spammy. But the general public may have a limit to what they accept as reasonable. In the aftermath of the Cambridge Analytica scandal, as well as due to the GDPR legislation discussed in the next section, the amount of data being recorded by Internet giants has come under scrutiny in the media. Journalists and others are now extracting the data Facebook, Google, and others store on them and their behavior, and are analyzing the data to understand how much personal information companies really track.

The results will amaze you. Brian X. Chen wrote an article called "I Downloaded the Information that Facebook Has on Me. Yikes." in the *New York Times*.[16] While that data was extensive, it turns out that the data Google kept on him was a full eight gigabytes, versus a 650 megabytes for Facebook. He writes "Google had a record of apps I had opened on an Android phone since 2015, along with the date and time," and also

16   Brian X. Chen. "I Downloaded the Information that Facebook Has on Me. Yikes.," *The New York Times*, 9 April 2018. *https://www.nytimes.com/2018/04/11/technology/personaltech/i-downloaded-the-information-that-facebook-has-on-me-yikes.html*

found out that "Facebook also had my entire phonebook, including the number to ring my apartment buzzer." Apparently, Facebook had given or sold his personal data—which could include email address, phone number, and more—to about 500 advertisers, many of which he had never heard of or been in contact with.

In a Gizmodo blog post in April 2018, David Nield notes, "As soon as you sign into Android with your Google account, your device gets linked to your Google credentials, and Google starts logging data such as the length and type of your phone calls, your phone's location, the device you're using, and more."[17]

We can expect a pushback from legislators and the public unless the industry treats personal information with a sufficient level of respect, security, and privacy. I believe most people are completely unaware of how much personal information companies track, and it can backfire into considerable bad-will, as was the case with Facebook in light of the Cambridge Analytica scandal.

In fact, entire countries are now using similar technologies. The Chinese government is currently launching a social ranking system that scores its citizens and monitors the behavior of its population. The social credit system, which was announced in 2014, claims that "keeping trust is glorious and breaking trust is disgraceful," according to a government document. The system is mandatory and is intended to be fully operational in 2020. Citizens with a poor social-credit rating are reportedly already being barred from planes and trains, as well as denied loans and government support. We might soon find ourselves in a version of George Orwell's *1984*.

Legal Matters and Explainable AI

Authorities are beginning to look into data privacy much more. A current example is the European Union's General Data Protection Regulation (GDPR), which came into force in May 2018. This law applies to any company, anywhere in the world, that store or process personal information on European citizens (even recording the TCP/IP address of

---

17   David Nield. "All the Ways Your Smartphone and Its Apps Can Track You," Gizmodo, 1 April 2018. *https://fieldguide.gizmodo.com/all-the-ways-your-smartphone-and-its-apps-can-track-you-1821213704*

anonymous website visitors in log files is considered to be personal data by GDPR).

Fines for misconduct are heavy, up to 20 million or 4% of the global corporate turnover, whichever is greater. That got the attention of business leaders, who need to mitigate this legal risk. In addition to a number of regulations on data storage, data processing, and data privacy, GDPR also regulates profiling and automated individual decision making, including AI and machine learning. Sensitive personal data, for example religious, political, sexual, or ethnic information, must in most cases not be used for decisions that cause legal effects, or decisions of similar importance.

However, even if you ensure that machine learning algorithms do not use this type of data, predictions or decisions can still be discriminatory, as such bias can be introduced indirectly from other data, either individually or when combined. For example, an AI bot may be less likely to give loans to people of a certain ethnic group. The machine learning solution or its developers may not be racist, but the skewed decisions may be derived from other socio-economic data, which is itself the product of systemic racism. The developers might not even be aware of this fact. In addition to being unethical, it may be illegal as well.

A well-known example is Microsoft's AI-powered Twitter chatbot Tay, which was launched in March 2016. It knew how to chat with people and learned from past chat correspondence sessions. Unfortunately, Tay was targeted by trolls who had racist discussions with it, and that language was integrated into its system. Tay became a vivid racist, spreading extremely offensive Nazi opinions. Microsoft had to shut down Tay after only sixteen hours.

Another example is an AI-driven beauty contest arranged by Beauty.ai that was found to predominantly choose white people as winners. Beauty.ai used large datasets of photos to build an algorithm that tried to assess beauty. The algorithm predicting the attractiveness was trained with too few images of people of color, thus biasing winners to white contestants. This wasn't intentional of course, but we will see more examples like this in the future. Companies developing their own AI solutions need to aware of this type of problem.

Due to the increased use of AI in safety-critical or otherwise sensitive purposes, as well as new legislation as outlined above, there is a need to introduce transparent AI models where the predictions or decisions can be explained afterwards. Deep neural network algorithms can make predictions that are hard or impossible to explain, even by their designers. To open the black box, we need to understand the decision making (transparency), the reasoning behind a particular decision (explainability), and the certainty behind decisions (provability).

An example is the self-driving Uber car that killed a woman in Tempe, Arizona, in March 2018. For a long time, people discussed what would happen when the first lethal accident happened with a self-driving car. Now it is a reality, and we cannot push such discussions to the future any longer. Researchers determined that the car's vision system recognized the pedestrian but the response may have been deferred or delayed due to other rules about how to respond to objects in the road.

Luckily, there is progress being made in explainable AI, also known as XAI or Transparent AI, and I believe legislation on this is likely to follow.

AI Apocalypse?

At the beginning of this book, we looked at some of the myths and misconceptions about AI. Now that we've looked at the technology in much more detail, let's return to that idea for a moment. Clearly, AI presents many opportunities for the future, but not everyone agrees. Some even warn that AI will be the end of humanity. Elon Musk, for example, frequently tweets about the risks of strong artificial intelligence and calls for legislation to control it. August 2017 he wrote, "If you're not concerned about AI safety, you should be. Vastly more risk than North Korea." In another tweet from 26 November 2017, he provides an alarming vision of the future of humanoid robots: "In a few years, that bot will move so fast you'll need a strobe light to see it. Sweet dreams."

Who should we believe, and are there real risks? No one knows, and only time will tell. One thing is for sure: AI will get smarter and more capable over time, and may even surpass human intelligence. Ray Kurzweil, whom we mentioned earlier, predicts this singularity (as he calls it) will happen in 2045.

In 2012, he was appointed director of engineering at Google, managing a team focusing on machine intelligence and natural language understanding. Prior to that, he was responsible for a number of achievements that gave him the National Medal of Technology from President Clinton in a White House ceremony. In his book *The Singularity is Near*, he writes, "By the time of Singularity, there won't be a distinction between humans and technology. This is not because humans will have become what we think of as machines today, but rather machines will have progressed to be like humans and beyond."

If true, Elon Musk might be right. This is scary stuff. This is why he calls for legislation to control AI before it is too late. However, we are far from such artificial intelligence right now. The kind of AI currently being deployed is narrow AI, which can only optimize certain problems to which they are specifically designed to handle. They can't do anything else. Strong or general AI is still far away, but who knows what advancements are made in a decade or two? Regardless, there are reasons to be cautious when it comes to strong AI and adopting a healthy dose of cautiousness can't be wrong.

Chapter Summary

In this chapter, I've elaborated on ethics and legal matters as they relate to AI and automated individual decision-making. These are important topics for anyone moving forward with using AI for decision-making based on personal data. I think society at large hasn't fully understood the consequences of an AI-world, and we will likely start to see legislators upgrading the legal frameworks in the future.

FINAL THOUGHTS

I thought about writing this book for a long time, and when I couldn't find any books that balanced actionable information for marketers and managers with the right amount of details, I decided it was time to get started and write the book myself. During the project, I met many nice people in the AI industry, but even more, I got a much deeper insight into how machine learning and predictive analytics can be used in almost every corner of our industry.

I am confident these new technologies will not only transform, but also disrupt, the marketing industry. This is why many corporations bet their future on AI. There are immense opportunities to be harvested now, but great risks for the laggards too. Managers should pay attention. Some companies might already be late to the party and will face an uphill battle to remain competitive. AI is likely to boost the winner-takes-all effect, and large corporations with lots of data may have an unfair advantage over new or smaller companies.

Marketing will be much more data-driven in the future, and thus much more reliant on software and other technology. This is not to say that the creative side will not be important in the future, but the marketing framework will be set by numerical analysis, behavior tracking, and software automation. AI-generated creative material based on data-driven insights may come sooner than we think. The industry is making leaps and bounds right now, and what was impossible two years ago is a fact today. The only thing for certain is that change is happening fast.

CMOs will thus need a completely different skillset and must be much more versed in data-driven decision-making and advanced software solutions. In fact, the marketing manager of the future might well need the skills of both CIOs and CTOs! Marketing technology will soon be the centerpiece of the marketing department.

Predictive marketing and machine-learning will transform the industry and enable personalized customer experiences that will make marketing relevant again. Spammy marketing outreach is no longer accepted, and the customer can be put at the center once more. The insights uncovered by AI algorithms are data-driven and can be based on information from humans or machines. In this new world, without data, there can be no insights. However, with large amounts of personal data come legal and ethical risks.

Already we have seen scandals with data breaches and abuse of personal information on a massive scale. Even the outcome of public elections may have been affected on both sides of the Atlantic. Legislators are reacting and trying to keep up, as we see with the European Union General Data Protective Regulation (GDPR).

I believe every marketer needs to be aware of what data-driven marketing, marketing automation, and artificial intelligence are, the basics of what they can do, and what effect they will have on marketing going forward. It they don't, they will soon be out of a job.

I hope this book has provided some insights into what is happening and what is possible today. Make your own conclusions, and act accordingly.

Once thing is for sure: marketing will never be the same again!

PLEASE REVIEW
THIS BOOK

I had a lot of fun writing this book, and I hope you found it interesting and useful. If you did, I would kindly ask you for a favor. If you want to support this and future projects, please write an honest review on Amazon.com and give it as many stars as you think it deserves: *https://www.amazon.com/Data-Driven-Marketing-Artificial-Intelligence-Predictive-ebook/dp/B07D7FD1YM*

I would be most grateful. If you have any feedback, good or bad, that you would like to share with me personally, you can fin my contact information at the end of the book.

APPENDIX 1: TRADITIONAL DATA-DRIVEN MARKETING

Even without AI, Internet marketing is already heavily data-driven. Forward-looking companies have used data-driven marketing and marketing automation for years, and these methods will only be increased as AI systems become more robust. Here, we cover some of the key aspects of traditional data-driven marketing to supplement our discussion of machine learning systems. While some of this material may be familiar to you, it's important to understand the basic technology upon which the latest AI tools are built.

Key Marketing Metrics

Many metrics can be applied to marketing, and I will highlight some of the most common ones traditionally used for data-driven marketing. If you are a marketer, you have likely come across several of these before.

Sales Indictors

It is often possible to track metrics that signal the likelihood of future sales. For software and cloud service companies, a key sales indicator may be the amount of people who sign up for a free thirty-day trial. This number can be measured over time and correlated to the actual sales that follow from the trial users.

For example, it might be that, on average, 5% of the trial users purchase the software or service within a month, and 1% of them purchase in the second month. By monitoring the number of trial users each month, you can get a good gauge on how the sales will be in the next month or two. Sales indicators in other industries might be the number of test drives a car dealer has each week, the number of free consultations a medical clinic has each month, or the number of people who attend a weekly sales webinar. Monitor the sales indicators most relevant to your company and industry, and you will be able to predict your future sales.

Predictive analytics can help you to design even better prediction systems, as you can then combine a large number of attributes, KPIs (Key Performance Indicators), and other metrics for a combined prediction of higher accuracy.

Churn

Churn is the percentage of customers who defect and stop purchase from you. It is a key indicator of customer loyalty and is often calculated on a yearly basis. If you monitor your churn rate, you can react to dropping loyalty by improving the customer experience or otherwise introduce changes that makes your product or company appear more attractive to your customers.

Churn is traditionally calculated on historical data, but with predictive marketing and machine learning, we can predict churn before it happens on a per-customer level. For example, we could be notified that a particular customer is 92% likely to defect in the next month. This gives us an opportunity for one final attempt to keep the customer. In general, reducing churn and keeping customers longer is a cost-effective way to improve revenue, as the average customer lifetime value goes up.

Customer Lifetime Value

Not all customers are equally valuable in most companies. They all purchase for different amounts and churn at different times. This is where Customer Lifetime Value (CLTV) calculations becomes useful. This tries to predict the total future value of a customer. It is impractical to consider CLTV for long periods (such as a teenager staying as a customer for fifty more years). In practice, it is best calculated for the next three to five years.

If you can predict the CLTV for all your individual customers, you know who your best and worst customers are, and you can adjust your marketing and customer experience accordingly. For example, you can step-up your service level for your best customers, and reduce ad spending for your low-spending customers. In general, you can use CLTV to build your marketing strategies and for segmentation for any number of purposes. Being a predictive metric, CLTV is well suited for predictive analytics and machine learning.

Internet Marketing and e-commerce

With Internet marketing comes a whole set of acronyms and new indicators, in particular related to search engine marketing (SEM), social media marketing (SMM), and e-commerce. Some of the most commonly used metrics in Internet marketing are:

- Cost Per Click (CPC): This metric is often used in online advertisements, where the advertiser does not pay for ad impressions, but rather the number of clicks on the ad. CPC is simply the average cost for each ad click that drives traffic to your landing page.

- Cost Per Mille (CPM): Less used nowadays as most advertisers prefer the CPC pricing model. CPM is the cost to get 1000 impressions of an online ad. CPM does not measure any tangible marketing result and is thus a weaker indicator than CPC.

- Click Through Rate (CTR): This is the percentage of people who can see a clickable ad or link, and actually clicks on it. It is simply the number of ad impressions divided by the number of clicks on it.

- Transaction Conversion Rate (TCR): This is the percentage of people who purchase after clicking through to your website from an online ad.

- Return on Ad dollars spent (ROA): This measures the financial efficiency of an ad by dividing the revenue generated by the cost of the ad campaign.

- Customer Acquisition Cost (CAC): The average cost of getting a new customer.

- Lead Acquisition Cost (LAC): The average cost of getting a new lead.

- Bounce rate (BR): This is the percentage of the website visitors who leaves the website immediately upon arriving to it. This is a measure of how engaging the landing page is to its visitors, alternatively, a measure of how well the website visitors matches your target audience.

- Conversion Rate (CR): The conversion rate of something is how well it performs its intended task, measured in percent of the total number of visitors. It can be many things, for example how many clicks a hypertext link or a call-to-action button, how many submit a registration form, how many add a product to the shopping cart, or how many complete the purchase.

In e-commerce, a few additional metrics are often monitored and used for data-driven marketing:

- Shopping cart abandonment rate: Unfortunately, it is common 70% or more of the customers that add a product to the shopping cart never complete the purchase. Shopping cart abandonment management is used to prevent this, and e-commerce companies monitor this measure.
- RFM analysis: By analyzing the recency, frequency, and monetary value (RFM) of each customer, it is possible to determine who are the best customers, who are at risk of defecting, and related insights. RFM analysis is a good example of an area where predictive machine learning algorithms probably can do a far better job.

If you are into paid online ads or e-commerce, you may want to monitor and react to the metrics mentioned in this section. They will signal what works and doesn't, and can help remove monetary waste or inefficiencies in your online business.

Predicting Customer Choice

When you plan to introduce new products, or new versions of existing products, understanding what customers want allows you to prioritize what features and capabilities to add or remove from the product plans. After all, it is rare a company can add everything under the sun to a product, for a whole lot reasons. Thus, you need to get better insights into how customers value different product parameters to make the optimum trade-offs.

You can use conjoint analysis for this; it is an advanced market research technique that unravels how customers really value different capabilities or product attributes, if they can't have them all. Conjoint analysis presents people with a number of choices and analyze the drivers for those choices. As such, it helps make data-driven decisions in terms of product development strategies and product roadmaps.

With better information on what product capabilities the market actually values, you can avoid investing in development of product features that doesn't help drive sales and optimize the product's capabilities such that it ticks the needs of as many potential customers as possible. This too is a kind of data-driven marketing, but for use by the product management team rather than traditional marketing.

Marketing Automation

Most companies who are at least somewhat up to speed with Internet marketing use marketing automation tools these days. If you are unfamiliar with the concept of marketing automation, the next few sections provide a crash course. If, on the other hand, you want to learn more on marketing automation, you can read my book, *Mastering Online Marketing,* available on Amazon and Apple iBooks, and other places.[18]

First, marketing automation systems commonly help attract more website visitors by supporting inbound content marketing. Features may include SEO keyword analytics, content strategy analysis, and blogging platforms. Marketing automation system tools help convert anonymous website visitors into known leads using lead generation assets such as call-to-action (CTA) buttons, landing pages with registration forms, thank you pages, and contact databases that often are synchronized with CRM systems as well.

Leads are nurtured automatically over time, using automated email sequences or other channels, until the leads are turned into customers or are lost. Once a lead becomes a customer, marketing automation software can continue to nurture those contacts into happier customers, and turn them into advocates for your business—evangelists. To help provide personalized experiences, marketing automation systems like HubSpot, Marketo, Pardot, and Eloqua track the behavior (digital footprint) of

18   *https://www.amazon.com/MASTERING-ONLINE-MARKETING-generation-automation/dp/1517057949*

leads and customers as they engage with the website and other online assets.

A core functionality in such systems is the capability to segment leads and customers based on various filter conditions, for example their demographics or behavioral data. This information is then used to determine who should get what content, at what time.

Traditional marketing automation systems often facilitate A/B testing of landing pages, call-to-action buttons (CTAs), and email. With A/B testing, you design two versions of the marketing asset you want to test, and the system deploy both and measure which version performs best (generates most form submissions, button clicks, or email opens). The winning version is then used going forward. This is data-driven decision making for the benefit of improved marketing results.

Marketing automation systems commonly can perform automated calculations of lead scores, thus estimating how close a particular lead is to purchase. Lead scores are traditionally calculated by assigning scores to activities like visiting a certain page, downloading a PDF, opening an email, and so on. Predictive lead scoring is now becoming popular, and it achieves the same thing using predictive analytics and machine learning. Such estimations help the sales organization prioritize what leads to focus on, or how to auto-nurture leads with email campaigns. We thus use data on each contact to assess their interest level.

Smart adaptive content is where the copy, images, banner-ads, call-to-action buttons, etc. are dynamically swapped for each website visitor or email recipient in real-time, based on data available on their digital footprint (behavior) or other segmentation data that is available, such as lifecycle stage, location, job title, or something else. Effectively, data attributes that can be used to derive the interests of a particular visitor is used to adapt the content.

It is important to note that while traditional marketing automation systems help nurture leads automatically using data-driven methodologies, this isn't the same as self-learning AI systems. They are merely automation robots that follow predefined workflow logic, and do not modify their own decision logic when the data they process changes. AI-based systems on the other hand, learn from new data and modify their behavior accordingly to do a better job over time.

Segmenting

Marketers have used segmentation to improve the precision of their marketing efforts since CRM-systems and databases came into use, and even before that. Segmentation can be used to target contacts better when campaigns are initiated for customer acquisition, up-selling and cross-selling, seasonal campaigns, retention, and more.

With segmentation, we find a sub-segment of all contacts in the database who all share attributes such that they all are more likely to be responsive to a particular marketing outreach than other contacts in the database. For example, your dentist in France may be less interested in an invitation to your seminar tour on yoga in Scandinavia than the Swedish yoga teachers in your database.

Segmentation can be done based on many factors, including demographics, geography, firmographics, past behavior online (digital footprint), purchase pattern, and more. With segmentation, campaigns become better targeted, thus improving their efficiency. You also appear more relevant by not reaching out to people unlikely to be interested in a particular offer. Since the decision to include or exclude someone from a campaign or offer is based on data from the contact database, this is data-driven marketing.

Behavior Tracking

Marketing automation system can "spy" on what visitors do on the webpage, whether they open or click on emails, how they watch movies, etc., down to the individual level. In effect, this is behavior tracking, or monitoring the digital footprint of visitors. This collection of data can then be used for data-driven decision logic with the aim of personalizing the marketing according to the assumed interest of each individual.

More specifically, it is often possible to track how:

- Visitors behave on the web pages
- What links and buttons they click
- What e-mail messages they open
- What links and buttons in emails they click
- How they watch video clips

This information may be used for data-driven marketing and personalization, where each person receives the right information at the right time. It can also be used by the sales team to assist in prioritization of what leads to spend valuable sales rep time on.

One of the basic features of marketing automation systems is the ability to follow what each visitor does on the site. The system simply instructs the company's website, blog, or landing pages to watch how they are used using a small tracking code. This is a win-win situation; the marketers get better results, and the customer gets relevant information at the right time—and less spam.

Initially, the system doesn't know an individual visitor's behavior, only that of the total visitors as a whole. However, when an anonymous visitor comes to a website for the first time, he or she is linked to a tracking cookie along with their computer's unique internet address. This tracks the person's behavior each time they visit the site, though their identity is still unknown. However, if the visitor uses an online form to sign up for an email newsletter, purchase a product, or access some other aspect of the site, the anonymous data collected with the tracking cookie is merged with the personalized data to create a profile.

User information can also be collected based on how they open and interact with emails sent from a company. If they click on links or buttons, this behavior is added to what the company already knows about them. By adding individualized links to each email, specific to each user, the company can track individual people based on their behavior.

Even further, it's possible to gather information on users based on how they watch online videos. Sites can track if a video is watched, how long it played, and whether it was fast-forwarded or replayed. While this may not seem connected to marketing, it can be used to change how a company presents information to its users to make that delivery more efficient and useful. All of this collected data further enables segmentation and personalization, making the marketing experience more effective.

For more information on behavior tracking in marketing automation systems, read my blog post: *https://unemyr.com/behavior-tracking-marketing-automation/*

Automated Workflows

As marketing automation systems track what known leads and customers do on the website, with emails, and more, it is possible to trigger automatic follow-up logic when someone has done something you have set as a trigger. In effect, you install trip-wires on the website that trigger context-specific follow-up sequences or nurturing logic. There are an enormous amount of examples of how certain behaviors can trigger marketing automation workflow logic, but just to mention a few:

- You have clicked on button X or hyperlink Y, so now we will email you Z emails on topic W in the next few weeks
- You have (or have not) opened email X, so now...
- You have (or have not) clicked on link X in email Y, so now...
- You have (or have not) downloaded PDF X, so now...
- You have (or have not) watched video X for more than 30 seconds, so now...
- You have (or have not) visited the blog in 30 days, so now...
- You have visited the pricing page, so now we notify the nearest distributor

The trigger events for this type of marketing automation workflow logic can also be combined with data fields we have on that particular lead in the database, for example:

- Buyer persona
- Segmenting data (industry, city, number of employees, title)
- Lifecycle stage in the customer journey
- Lead score
- Past purchase history
- Birthday

Using such data as a trigger condition would lead to nurturing workflows like these being started for the leads that qualify:

- You are now classified as persona type X, so now...
- You live in city X and have job title Y, so now...
- You are in the decision stage, so now...

- Your lead score is >25%, so now we send X emails with a soft sales message
- Your lead score is >50%, so now we send X emails with a hard sales message
- Your lead score is >75%, so now we schedule a sales rep to call you

Taking this one step further, you can combine this with data you get from integrations with other IT systems.

Integrating Data from Other Systems

While a marketing automation system is useful on its own, it is even better to integrate it with other IT systems used at the company, for example e-commerce platforms, ERP-systems, CRM-systems, digital logistic systems, customer support systems, webinar platforms, or proprietary internal IT systems.

With such integrations, workflow logic can be triggered also by considering data like:

- You have (or have not) registered for webinar X, so now...
- You did (or did not) attend webinar X, so now...
- You have (or have not) purchased anything in the webshop for three months, so now...
- You left the shopping cart without checking out, so now...
- You contacted customer service last week, so now...
- You have purchased for $5000, so now...
- You have now used 95% of the disk space you have purchased, so now...
- You have now sent 1000 emails using our email service, so now...
- You have now used feature X of our software Y times, so now...
- You have now sent your first delivery to Canada, so now...
- The recipient of parcel X has now received the package, so now...

Let's see how we can use this for automation of smart management of a webinar, intended for hot leads in California. First, we create a marketing automation workflow that enrolls all leads located in California who have a lead score above 50%. Any contacts in the database who are already paying customers are excluded, as only leads are enrolled. This workflow starts by sending one email inviting the selected segment of leads to the webinar. The workflow then waits four days and sends a second invitation email—but only to those who didn't open the first invitation email. Why? To not wear out the leads who did in fact open the first invitation. They aren't likely to register for the webinar only because we spam them with reminders.

As a result of invitation email one or two, some people sign up using a webinar system that is integrated to the marketing automation system (you can do this, for example, using GotoWebinar and HubSpot). We then create a second workflow, that enrolls everyone who have registered for this webinar. This workflow sends an email to the registrants one day, and one hour, before the webinar to remind them to attend.

The workflow then waits until one day after the webinar, and the workflow then uses *if...then...else* logic to send different follow-up emails to those of the registered attendees who did in fact turn up to the webinar, and those who didn't. For those who did attend, you can send a few nurturing emails pushing them towards a purchase, and for the registered leads who never attended the webinar, send a few nurturing emails that try to make them join the next webinar instead, or at least offer them to watch the webinar recording.

This is a simple example of how marketing automation logic can use data-driven facts (segmentation, lead scoring, email opens, webinar registrations, and webinar attendance) to adjust the marketing message and nurture leads differently in a context-specific way.

Using External Data

You can even integrate data from external public web services and add that to the trigger condition for certain workflows. For example, you can connect to the local weather service using an API (application programming interface) and query the weather in a particular city for the coming weekend.

If you run a clothing shop, your automated weekend email promotion can then adapt itself to the weather situation. Promote swim gear in case of nice weather, and other products if it is going to rain, and perhaps do it differently in multiple cities with different weather that weekend. You can combine these trigger conditions and build a large amount of automated follow-up workflows, each performing highly tuned context-specific nurturing logic when a lead triggers each enrollment condition.

A more complex example would be to send a sequence of five marketing emails during the coming month to CEOs based in California who have over a thousand employees and have a lead score over 50%, if they did not open a particular email, and only if the company has sent over a hundred deliveries to Canada. You get the point. These examples showcase different types of context-specific lead nurturing triggered by automated and data-driven decisions.

By designing many different and highly targeted nurturing campaigns, you get a virtual sales rep that automatically nurtures leads in a relevant and timely way. It can cope with thousands of leads every minute, works 24/7, and never take breaks or goes on holiday. This type of data-driven marketing works nicely without AI, but as we saw earlier in the book, artificial intelligence can create many interesting tricks well beyond this.

APPENDIX 2:
VENDOR
INTERVIEWS

When talking to some CEOs and marketing managers I know about my book project, it became clear that because AI in marketing is such a new field, many business leaders interested in using these technologies don't know where to start. Several managers mentioned they in particular wanted to know more about what commercial solutions there are on the market for purchase, and what these products can do in more detail.

To address this, I have added this bonus chapter including sections of my interviews with a number of vendors of AI-based marketing tools. As mentioned earlier, I am not associated or affiliated with any of these vendors, and I get no financial benefits from highlighting them. Including a vendor in this book or on my website does not mean that I endorse them.

In this chapter, I provide a sneak peek, in alphabetic order, of the vendor interviews I provide to complement this book. To read them in full, please visit my blog at *www.unemyr.com/blog.*

Albert

Albert is a digital marketing automation platform based on an artificial intelligence engine that focuses on ad purchase and campaign optimization.

CEO of Albert Technologies, Inc., Or Shani, identified that marketing is still far too manual, even with modern tools, and often requires extensive human interaction. To fix this, his company created Albert, a fully autonomous digital marketer. The artificial intelligence tool provides services once delivered by a marketing team, including managing and executing self-driven digital marketing campaigns.

When I spoke with Or, he explained that Albert is able to execute marketing strategies quickly and at scale by wading through vast amounts of data. Or argues that this allows the marketing team to focus on high-level strategies and creative solutions.

Customers provide Albert with their business goals, KPIs, and known audience data, and the program creates a campaign specific to each marketer's strategy and unique audience. Using learning algorithms, Albert is able to refine these efforts as they develop. The technology requires limited upfront input or ongoing management, and will run hundreds of campaign variants to maximize effectiveness.

Read the full interview: *https://unemyr.com/albert-marketing-ai/*

Bookmark

Bookmark is a website building company that uses AI to build unique websites for each user, bypassing the template-model used by its competitors.

Many website builders use common templates that are easy to use, but result in sites that all look alike. Bookmark allows non-technical users to create individualized sites without the need to learn to code or be fluent in the design and layout process.

Bookmark users are introduced to AiDA, their Artificial Intelligence Design Assistant. After defining their business type and name, and a few other details, users are presented with an AI-generated site for review, complete with unique images, pages, sections, and layout. If they don't like it, they can ask for a new version, and the system creates one in thirty seconds. When they're ready, uses can then publish the site and use Bookmark's training modules to learn promotion strategies like developing a brand identity and marketing on social media.

In an interview with Naser Alubaidi, Head of Marketing at Bookmark, he explained that AiDA uses genetic algorithms, machine learning, and some human-assisted elements to create unique websites specific to each user's needs. The machine learning elements also mean that the system learns from each project, allowing it to make better predictions on how to create a suitable site for each user.

Read the full interview: *https://unemyr.com/bookmark-ai-webdesign/*

Conversica

Conversica provides an AI Sales Assistant that helps companies find and secure customers more quickly and efficiently by automatically contacting, engaging, qualifying, and following up with leads via natural, two-way conversations.

Following up with potential customers and separating good from bad leads takes a huge amount of time for a sales team, but automating some of that work allows them to focus on closing deals. The company was founded in 2007 and now provides AI-driven lead engagement software for marketing and sales organizations.

I spoke with Gary Gerber, Senior Director and Head of Product Marketing at Conversica. He explained that the company's automated sales assistants are built on a proven AI platform integrating natural language processing (NLP), natural language generation (NLG), and machine learning (ML) capabilities and engage prospects over multiple communication channels and in multiple languages. The result is a system that can reach out to and follow up with every lead by engaging them with natural two-way "human" conversation. Gerber argues that this creates far more "at bats" to be managed by sales reps, leading to more closed deals. He sees this as the future of automation: "Today, AI is about empowering humans to do better work. Tomorrow, it's going to be about the AI interacting and taking a lot of things off our plate so that we can live better lives."

Read the full interview: *https://unemyr.com/conversational-ai-coversica/*

Cortex

Cortex uses AI and machine learning to create marketing content at any scale with high precision for each user's audience.

I spoke to Brennan White, Co-founder and CEO of Cortex, to learn more about the company. He explained that while at a previous company, he noticed problems with his team being able to plan, produce, and distribute creative deliverables at scale. He also noticed that no other companies were addressing this issue. The result was a new company based on a system that uses machine learning to change how creative decisions are made.

Cortex uses marketing content from tens of thousands of brands and campaigns. Then, using machine learning and AI, the system enriches that data to determine which aspects of a creative design have the most impact on brands and their specific goals. It then creates a calendar of marketing content spanning a few months and prompts the human marketer for feedback and approval.

White says that this system allows companies to maximize their ROI from content marketing, often within six months. While the software automates much of the grunt work involved in creating content, several approval steps also allow the team to add material from sources unavailable to the program, like meetings and personal communication. This ensures that the system helps the human team without overriding their creative decisions.

Read the full interview: *https://unemyr.com/cortex-ai-social-media-content/*

Crayon

Crayon is a market and competitive intelligence platform that enables businesses to track, analyze, and act on everything about their competitors.

CMO Ellie Mirman explained recently that businesses today often have great visibility internally, with extensive data on things like sales, product metrics, and strategies. Crayon, she says, helps businesses generate the same type of information about markets, competitors, and customers.

Crayon's system monitors millions of webpages, watching carefully for changes that may signal a competitor's actions. Mirman notes that often the most important competitor data isn't what they publish, but can be learned through subtle website changes or new customer reviews. The system uses machine learning and analyst curation to sift through the data it collects. The company then provides uses with tools to analyze and interact with the data to stay on top of changes in their industry.

Read the full interview: *https://unemyr.com/crayon-market-competitor-intelligence-ai/*

Crimson Hexagon

Crimson Hexagon's consumer insights platform is used by commercial clients to understand audiences, track brand perception and campaign performance, and detect competitive and market trends.

The company offers a SaaS platform for analyzing large-scale consumer conversations so clients can build a more complete view of the customer. For example, companies can monitor what is being said about them online, and understand the causes behind spikes in attention, either positive or negative.

I spoke with Jane Zupan, Senior Director of Product Marketing at Crimson Hexagon, about their system. She explained that the tool monitors publically available channels like social media, company ratings and reviews, and other media attention. It then uses four concepts—AI, a broad data library, image analytics, and role-based used experience—to create an interactive picture of a brand's performance online.

Read the full interview: *https://unemyr.com/social-media-analytics-crimson-hexagon/*

Crobox

Crobox analyzes shoppers' behavior (e.g., click-through, add-to-cart, and check out data) in response to specific persuasive messaging. The system then uses psychographic data to explain the psychological tendencies of individuals.

Janelle de Weerd, Marketing Manager at Crobox, explained that companies have long had detailed demographic, behavioral, and transactional data at their disposal. Their innovation was to provide missing information about motivation and the personality profiles of shoppers. She argues that by influencing shoppers to act at each step in the buyer's journey, the company can provide tangible value to clients.

de Weerd says that her company's approach is "derived from behavioral psychology, optimized by AI." Their system use machine learning algorithms to interpret behavioral data from shoppers on specific platforms. It first learns what products are more effective at triggering user actions, and then matches the best persuasive message to that product. The company then provides clients with an in-depth report about their customers' psychographic profiles, allowing for better targeting and marketing strategies that work best in triggering online behavior.

Read the full interview: *https://unemyr.com/crobox-behavior-psychology-ecommerce/*

Cubed.ai

CUBED is a marketing analytics platform that helps businesses understand their performance across the full consumer journey, including multi-visit and multi-device interactions.

Russell McAthy, Founder and CEO of CUBED, explains that the system uses a linear regression model. They look at every successful event, or conversion, to understand what happened prior to that sale. This analysis includes data points from across the user's experience, including impressions, emails, web visits and even retail store sales data. It then uses machine learning to train an algorithmic attribution model to best understand the individual touch points impacting consumers.

McAthy argues that rather than using artificial intelligence, the system uses what he calls attribution intelligence, since humans are still integral to the process. The company uses this system to provide a level of granularity that enables marketers to make small adjustment towards large business goals.

Read the full interview: *https://unemyr.com/cubed-attribution-modeling/*

Dynamic Yield

Dynamic Yield is a personalization technology company that aims to empower marketers to serve indiviualized digital experiences to customers at scale.

I spoke to Mike Mallazzo, Head of Content at Dynamic Yield. He explained that the company's founder, Liad Agmon, was frustrated by the inability of publishers to create unique experiences for different customers. His goal was to create a better experience for users across verticals.

The company uses machine learning and big data to determine which variations of marketing outreach work best for each user, and then automatically allocate traffic to higher performing variations. Using predictive targeting, the system them proactively identifies opportunities to provide users with more relevant experiences that boost revenue and engagement. They also give marketers access to an interface that can personalize experiences, serve product recommendations, and automatic optimization.

Read the full interview: *https://unemyr.com/personalization-ai-dynamic-yield/*

Emarsys

Scaling and personalization are two of the most important issues facing marketing today. Emarsys offers a cloud-based marketing platform that allows AI-based personalization across channels, including email, SMS, web, offline, and IoT devices.

I spoke with Lindsay Tjepkema, Global Head of Content at Emarsys. She explains that their system differs from most other products that offer personalization within each channel. Instead, they calculate personalization based on a single customer's demographics and behavior, and the AI then identifies the best channel and message to connect with them.

The platform consolidates all data about a user gathered from the web, email, and purchase information to create a customer profile that grows as more information is gathered. This profile can then be adjusted and applied to marketing outreach using Emarsys' cloud-based platform.

Read the full interview: *https://unemyr.com/emarsys-marketing-personalization/*

Ignite

Ignite Technologies offers a tool called Infer that estimates how likely someone is to buy, based on their similarities in their demographic or behavioral information to actual customers.

Infer uses machine learning and predictive lead scoring to compare the past behavior of people who later became customers. This is then compared to people who have not yet purchased from the company to establish who is likely to buy. Marketing outreach can then be adjusted to help transition them from lead to customer.

In my interview with Ingite's Vice President of Professional Services, Rob Franks, he explained that the system pulls data from over 4000 sources to understand customer behavior. This information is analyzed to create a score for each person based on the likelihood that they will become a customer. This provides sales teams current information on each lead, allowing them to focus on opportunities with the highest probability of closing.

Read the full interview: *https://unemyr.com/ignite-infer-predictive-lead-scoring/*

Lexalytics

The Lexalytics Intelligence Platform was developed to help company's work better with text online. Using five modules, the company processes, analyzes, and provides insights around company data like surveys, and social media posts. They offer a cloud-based API that integrates with third-party platforms like apps and MS Excel.

I spoke with Seth Redmore, the CMO at Lexalytics. He argues that there is too much human communication in the world today to understand, analyze, and act on without AI assistance. The company focuses on text found online, particularly conversational text that can hold layers of subtle meaning. This is difficult for other AI systems to interpret, but the focus on syntax, semantics, and context allows the system to understand adapt to online material. Redmore claims their system differs from other companies by using a hybrid of machine learning and other code, making their system tunable but powerful, and able to adapt quickly to different goals.

Read the full interview: *https://unemyr.com/lexalytics-text-sentiment-analysis/*

MarketMuse

MarketMuse uses AI to build content briefs that show how to write about a topic comprehensively, and how to tweak content to improve results. This allows marketers to write effective content on topics related to their business.

In an interview with Aki Balogh, founder and CEO of MarketMuse, he claims that this results in enhanced organic website traffic, improved thought leadership, and increased conversion rates. The system targets three types of people: content decision makers, content marketers, and SEO specialists. It creates a model of a topic and helps marketers write articles with the most relevant concepts and keywords to give it traction online and higher visibility in search engines.

The MarketMuse system works by scouring massive amounts of content from the web to look for coverage of the specified topic. It then helps marketers write about it just like a subject matter expert. It then calculates a content quality score to compare the piece to others online to help it stand out in Google rankings.

Read the full interview: *https://unemyr.com/ai-content-marketing-mar-ketmuse/*

Motiva

Motiva uses automated AI systems and machine learning to help optimize online marketing campaigns. Co-founder and CEO David Gutelius says that while many companies offer deep data mining services to increase campaign effectiveness, his company's goal is different. By focusing on listening rather than digging into user data, they aim to change the way marketing and advertising is done.

Gutelius says that rather than treat customers as only a potential transaction, their system aims to listen, learn, and serve. To do that, the company offers marketing and communications technologies geared to building trusting relationships in both B2B and B2C contexts, as well as governments, non-profits, and other organizations.

The system uses machine learning to analyze marketing campaigns to find the most compelling options and demonstrable results. The automated aspect of the platform automatically shifts campaign investment away from lower to higher performing messages, allowing a campaign to adapt to consumers instantly.

Read the full interview: *https://unemyr.com/motiva-ai-marketing-cam-paign-optimization/*

Narrative Science

Narrative Science helps enterprise companies use storytelling techniques to drive better business decisions. Their product, Quill, is a Natural Language Generation (NLG) platform using artificial intelligence to create natural, human-sounding narrative writing.

I spoke with Aimee Rowland, Director of Product Marketing. She said their software focuses on three attributes: relevance, to provide the best insights for each audience; intuition, to generate human-like, conversational language; and timeliness, to update whenever there is a change in the data to create updated, audience-specific narratives.

The platform combines natural language generation with the AI's analytical, reasoning, and learning capabilities to identify the most important insights and context behind the data.

Read the full interview: *https://unemyr.com/narrative-nlg-ai/*

Nudge.ai

Artificial intelligence in marketing goes beyond creating articles and monitoring social media. Nudge.ai helps sales teams build and maintain relationships by mapping and analyzing connections in an individual's extended network. It enables businesses to access new target accounts through their extended network and to analyze deal risk through precise relationship strength measurement.

In our recent conversation, Steve Woods, co-founder and CTO, said Nudge.ai provides a comprehensive relationship intelligence solution for organizations. The system allows sales representatives to see a firm's entire history with an account or prospect, which helps to avoid missed opportunities or awkward conversations. Its AI uses key reminders on each account to ensure the relationship is maintained, and enables sales teams to identify high-risk accounts to provide more attention. Rather than relying on traditional metrics, Nudge instead utilizes a team's ability to grow relationships and build trust through interactions with their accounts.

Read the full interview: *https://unemyr.com/nudge-prospecting-relationship-intelligence/*

Ometria

Ometria is a marketing platform that aims to help retailers better understand interact with their customers.

Ivan Mazour, CEO and Founder, says its mission is to help retailers create marketing experiences their customers will love. The key to this, he says, is not just to understand customers, but also to communicate with them in a way that makes them feel special, and keeps them coming back.

To accomplish this, Ometria plugs into retail and ecommerce platforms and aggregates data on customer touch points. Data on individual customers is collated and analyzed by their AI system to determine the best action to take through a marketing campaign. The system them uses direct marketing tools like personalized newsletters, triggered emails, and social media ads to reach leads, and provides marketing teams with the tools to optimize cross-channel campaigns.

Read the full interview: *https://unemyr.com/ometria-retail-marketing-ai/*

Outlier.ai

Outlier watches all data on a business and provides insights on unexpected changes in customer behavior, demographics, and conversions to help optimize marketing strategies.

I spoke with the co-founder and CEO of Outlier, Sean Byrnes. He noted that missing a shift in consumer preferences can cost company's millions of dollars, but with so much data to manage, it's impossible for humans to stay ahead of it. Rather than tasking a company with the large job of consolidating all of their data in one place, the Outlier system attaches to any point in the network, be it a cloud service or SQL database. It then uses machine learning to find insights across and between systems without input from the user.

Byrnes explains that Outlier uses a dozen forms of statistical machine learning in an eight-stage processing pipeline that converts raw metrics into human-readable insights. This involves paring down the amount of data that the user has to sift through in order to make the process as effective and efficient as possible.

Read the full interview: *https://unemyr.com/ai-business-data-outlier/*

Pathmatics

Pathmatics provides companies with data and analysis on their digital advertising campaigns, including who is buying how much, on which sites, and through which services.

Ken Roberts, Head of Marketing at Pathmatics, says that their system can be thought of as an advanced search engine for ads. They produce reports that allow readers to view data by advertiser, by site, by ad tech, and across custom time frames by tracking desktop display, pre-roll video, mobile web, native ad networks, and paid social advertising.

This allows brands to know when competitors launch new ad campaigns, and then understand if they are being outspent. The result is the ability to identify opportunities for existing and new clients and partners. Pathmatics uses an AI system that creates what Roberts calls "ad paths" that show the ad tech intermediaries on every impression.

Read the full interview: *https://unemyr.com/ai-ad-intelligence-pathmatics/*

Perfect Price

Perfect Prie is an artificial intelligence company focused on solutions for dynamic pricing.

Alexander Shartsis is co-founder and CEO of Perfect Price. He explained when I spoke with him recently that in today's world, consumers accept or even expect price fluctuations for some products (think airline tickets or car rentals). Using AI, software can monitor the market, including availability and demand, to help pinpoint the best price point at any given time. Perfect Price automates the complex task of sifting through this data to make dynamic pricing possible for any business.

The system combines several aspects of artificial intelligence, including supervised machine learning, clustering, and more. This allows segmentation to happen on a micro scale—each car at each location, for example—which saves the company money while also providing customers with the most competitive price.

Read the full interview: *https://unemyr.com/predictive-pricing-ai-perfect-price/*

Scoop.it

The scoop.it platform was first built in 2011 to help marketing professionals curate, create, and distribute content with the goal of creating measureable results and ROI. The company later added a B2B offering, and an AI enabled platform that helps marketers analyze and measure web content.

This AI system, called Hawkeye, indexes the web's editorial content on a huge range of media websites and industry blogs. Each piece is given a score by the system to measure its performance. Users can then access this data to help develop their own highly engaging content, and promote it using the more effective strategies.

I spoke with Guillaume Decugis, co-founder and CEO. He notes that today, marketers have to compete for attention from a larger range of other companies. This makes it crucial to have an AI-enabled system to help analyze what works, what doesn't, and how to best optimize content before and after publication.

Read the full interview: *https://unemyr.com/ai-content-marketing-strategy-scoop/*

Sentient Technologies

This company offers two main products in its digital marketing suite: Sentient Aware and Sentient Ascend. The former uses deep learning to understand the visual nature of a product catalog and combines that with data captured from user behavior. The latter is a conversion rate testing and optimization solution that allows uses to go beyond simple A/B testing to explore thousands of marketing ideas in the same time.

I spoke to Jeremy Miller, Vice President of Marketing. He explains that the system goes right down to the nuts and bolts, and tests even tiny aspects of a webpage like button and text color. This allows designs to be optimized for conversions and user interaction.

Read the full interview: *https://unemyr.com/sentient-cro-ai-conversion/*

Smart Moderation

Smart Moderation helps companies avoid negative online reviews, undesirable situations, and other risks that threaten a brand's prestige online.

Ciler Ay is the co-founder and CEO of Smart Moderation. I spoke with her about her company's use of AI and how the technology will change the world of marketing in the future. She explained that the platform is based on the idea that everyone should be free to express themselves online without facing trolling, profanity, offensive content, and other abuse. It uses artificial intelligence to monitor posts on social media and comment boards and automatically removes spam, unwanted ads, personal information, profanity, and abusive language, allowing real comments to drive the discussion. The system uses machine learning and natural language processing to understand text just like a human moderator.

Read the full interview: *https://unemyr.com/smart-moderation-brand-ai/*

TalkWalker

Talkwalker is a social listening and analytics company that helps brands and agencies to optimize the impact of their communication efforts.

Christophe Folschette is co-founder of Talkwalker. When I spoke with him recently, he explained that while companies like Google transformed internet searching, there was no real way to analyze social media posts effectively. Their software is a social media crawling platform that helps readers understand their information at any scale.

The platform allows companies to search social media, news sites, blogs, and forums for data relevant to their operations. It then allows analysis based on engagement level, sentiment, demographics, and location to help companies protect their online reputation, measure marketing performance, and promote products.

Read the full interview: *https://unemyr.com/talkwalker-social-analytics-ai/*

Vestorly

Vestorly is an AI-driven platform that curates content and sends it in personalized emails on behalf of marketers. Its AI-powered system uses a content search engine to crawl and index the internet in real time. It then aggregates and organizes stories, videos, and news. When a company uses the software and adds a contact list, the system recommends stories most likely to engage each reader.

I spoke with Anna Huston at Vestorly about the company's platform. She claims the individualized approach to email marketing can increase engagement rates, leading to reduced marketing costs, stronger client relationships, and better lead generation. By sharing content with millions of readers and analyzing the billions of data points that result, the system uses machine learning to constantly improve, allowing companies to target more specific demographics with precision.

Read the full interview: *https://unemyr.com/ai-curated-content-vestorly/*

To read more of my interviews with these industry leaders, go to my blog at *www.unemyr.com/blog.*

SUPERCHARGE
YOUR PROJECTS

Introducing new technology into a business is often quite hard due to a lack of resources, skills, or a combination of both. This is where experienced consultants come in. As a specialist in online marking, I offer help with setting up marketing automation or launching your own custom-designed AI software development projects. You can hire me directly for consulting services or outsource a project to my team and me.

I work as a marketing technologist, tech writer, and public speaker, and I live and breathe the latest trends in online promotion. I have over twenty years of experience using cutting-edge tools for promotion, as vice president of sales and marketing at an international firm, and speaking at industry conferences around the world. I am also the author of *Mastering Online Marketing*, an essential introduction and reference to building a world-class online marketing system using today's best tools. I know the industry, and understand the best ways to amplify your company's marketing strategy.

My business covers three areas: management advisory services, marketing program consulting, and custom AI development. I work with clients to find the best blend of these services for their situation and budget. In management advisory services, I serve as consulting chief marketing officer or digital marketing manager to advise boards and management teams on how to envision and enable a digital transformation strategy for the company.

Often, senior managers are aware of the types of changes they want to make but need a trusted senior advisor to help navigate the process. Digital transformation can mean different things to different companies. I have the experience to help you conceive and implement the right digital strategy for your industry and company situation.

For marketing program consulting, I work with your marketing department to analyze the current program and make recommendations on how to implement a data-driven marketing program. I focus on:

- Marketing automation and AI tools strategy
- Content strategy development

I help to develop a personalized outreach strategy using adaptive content and lead scoring to ensure the right message hits every applicable demographic. My job is to use the latest tools to automate this system and optimize your lead conversion.

After the initial setup, your system will run around the clock with minimal maintenance to bring a constant stream of traffic to your site. Software robots will intelligently recycle your highest-performing content to give them the greatest impact. The result is quality leads in your sales funnel to give your team the highest chance of making a sale.

Finally, I offer custom AI software development. In some cases, existing AI and machine learning tools can meet your needs with minor adaptation. However, some of my clients need custom developed AI solutions for their business. This can range from chatbot development to specialized machine learning systems. My background in software development and project management allows me to add significant value in this area. I apply a standardized software development process that includes requirements analysis, system flow charts, coding, testing, and deployment.

Should you be interested in these services for your company, please contact me at *magnus@unemyr.com*.

FEEDBACK
AND CONTACTING
THE AUTHOR

I hope you have found this book interesting, and while I have made every effort to provide as much valuable and error-free information as possible, no product is ever perfect.

If you have any feedback, good or bad, I would appreciate it very much if you would share it with me. With reader feedback, I can improve future versions of this book for the benefit of other readers. I can be contacted by email at *magnus@unemyr.com*.

For more information on my other books and services, visit my website and blog at *www.unemyr.com*.

ACKNOWLEDGEMENTS

I would like to thank my wonderful partner Anita for being understanding during all the late nights and weekends it took to write this book.

Other big thanks go to Martin Wass, who contributed the chapter on AI algorithms. You have made the book much better. Additionally, I want to thank my parents and brother for being supportive and teaching me the value of consistent hard work.

Finally, I would like to thank Eric Anderson at Chromoschema. com for the great editing services, Bogdan Matei for the cover art design and print version formatting, and Stephen Martin for the reviews of my drafts. Big thanks also to the industry leaders who agreed to be interviewed.

Without you, this book would not have been possible.

Thank you!

35588568R00135

Made in the USA
San Bernardino, CA
12 May 2019